Making and Breaking the Rules

Making and Breaking the Rules:

Women in Quebec, 1919-1939

Andrée Lévesque

translated by

Yvonne M. Klein

Making and Breaking the Rules
Andrée Lévesque

Éditions du remue-ménage

La norme et les déviantes
© Les Éditions du remue-ménage, Montréal
Dépôt légal, deuxième trimestre 1989
Bibliothèque nationale du Québec
Bibliothèque nationale du Canada

© 1994 Andrée Lévesque
Translation © 1994 Yvonne M. Klein

Canadian Cataloguing in Publication Data

Lévesque, Andrée

Making and breaking the rules: women in Quebec, 1919-1939

(The Canadian social history series)
Translation of: La norme et les déviantes: des femmes au Québec pendant l'entre-
deux-guerres.
Includes bibliographical references and index.
ISBN 0-7710-5283-9

1. Women – Quebec (Province) – Sexual behaviour – History – 20th century.
2. Women – Quebec (Province) – Conduct of life – History – 20th century.
3. Motherhood – Quebec (Province) – History – 20th century. 3. Prostitution –
Quebec (Province) – History – 20th century. I. Title. II. Series.

HQ1459.Q8L4813 1994   306.7′082   C93-094889-0

The translation of the text was completed with the support of the Canada Council.

This book has been published with the help of a grant from the Social Science
Federation of Canada, using funds provided by the Social Sciences and Humanities
Research Council of Canada.

McClelland & Stewart Inc.
The Canadian Publishers
481 University Avenue
Toronto, Ontario
M5G 2E9

1 2 3 4 5   98 97 96 95 94

Typesetting by M&S
Printed and bound in Canada by Webcom Ltd.

Contents

List of Tables and Figures / 6

Foreword / 7

1 The Norm / 11

2 Motherhood / 23

3 Sexuality / 53

4 "Deviance" / 74

5 The Rejection of Motherhood / 81

6 Wages of Sin: Unwed Mothers / 101

7 Commercial Sex: Prostitution / 117

Conclusion / 136

Notes / 140

Index / 157

List of Tables and Figures

Table 1. Female Criminality: Women Convicted as a Percentage of Total Convictions / 79

Table 2. Convictions of Keepers and Inmates of Bawdy Houses as a Percentage of Female Convictions, Quebce, 1928-1939 / 80

Table 3. Illegitimate Births, Quebec, 1926-1939 / 102

Table 4. Report on the Medical Examination of Persons Arrested in Disorderly Houses, Montreal, 1928-1939 / 139

Figure 1. Infant Mortality, Quebec, 1919-1939 / 31

Figure 2. Convictions for Serious Offences, Quebec, 1919-1939 / 75

Figure 3. Birth Rate per 1,000, Quebec, 1919-1939 / 82

Figure 4. Summary Convictions in Police Court of Women "Found-ins," Quebec, 1919-1939 / 118

Figure 5. Convictions for Offences Subject to Jury Trial: "Brothels, Madams, and Inmates," Women, Quebec, 1919-1939 / 132

Foreword

There is theory and then there is real life. There is prescribed behaviour and then there is what people actually do. Women's history lends itself to the study of the extent to which actual practice conforms to the ideal, and how far it departs from it. Do women always conform to the model imposed on them? What happens to those who violate the rules and the conventions? These questions have fascinated me throughout my years of teaching and research. At the outset, my project was very ambitious: I would undertake to analyse the theory of appropriate feminine behaviour in every aspect of women's lives in the years between the First World War and the Second World War. I quickly had to trim my sails. Since reproduction constitutes women's specific mission, and sexuality, so closely linked to reproduction, equally defines what is particularly female, these two themes imposed themselves as the organizing principles of the entire work. I had quickly to abandon, for example, everything that might have been said or written about women's work or political action, at least as far as these activities were independent of reproduction or sexuality.

I have tried to place in its historical context language that today we might find amusing or even ridiculous. It should be possible to produce a feminist, deconstructionist reading of the discourse that goes beyond mere condemnation. As an historian, I wished to avoid the expectation that previous generations should have possessed the reflexes and attitudes current today. As a feminist, however, I cannot prevent myself from denouncing sexist and discriminatory language, standards, and sanctions.

Public discourse transmits only a partial vision of reality and I wished to concentrate my attention on the lives of women. Since information on the demography, occupations, and experience of the majority of women may be found in more general works, I shall not repeat here what exists elsewhere; I am more interested in presenting a number of examples of non-conformity or marginal behaviour – that is, behaviour that deviates from the accepted norm.

Even when the public discourse is well documented, the study of deviance poses certain problems. I would have liked to augment the written sources with the testimony of women of the period. Conversations, rather than interviews, with elderly women have confirmed what I have learned from the written record. It is not difficult to find women who lived their lives according to the moral, social, and religious rules and standards of their day, but I was reluctant to detail once again the experiences of those who, in defying those norms, found themselves marked as "deviant." The majority of these women prefer to bury the past; we must respect their privacy.

Behind the statistics and the reports, the official sources retain a peculiar eloquence. The judicial archives teem with information about all the offences that came to the attention of the justice system – minutes of the depositions of witnesses and defendants, lawyers' defence pleas, speeches from the bench to juries all inform us not merely about criminal history and the administration of justice, but also about the social expectations of various interested parties. At the time that I was consulting these dusty scribblers and their often fragile files, there was no space at all provided to pursue this work, and I am grateful to M. Chalifoux for having found me a little corner in the basement of the courthouse in Montreal, and especially to Pierre Cousineau, of the Centre de pré-archivage of the Ministry of Justice, for his patience in unearthing all of these documents for me. I was unable to obtain the archives of Recorder's Court until the adjunct clerk of the Municipal Court, Alphonse Pelletier, directed me to the water treatment plant in Ville LaSalle, where masses of documents, including many dealing with prostitution, are preserved. I would like to thank Mr. Pelletier for his valuable assistance. In the same vein, Gisèle Marinier at the Municipal Archives of the city of Montreal provided me with important help by digging up the minutes of the 1924-25 Coderre Police Commission, when for two years I had been assured that this body of ten volumes did not exist.

Access to the registers and medical records of patients at the Hôpital de la Miséricorde presented certain problems in view of the confidential character of the information. After having assured the authorities of the Board of Directors of the Jacques Viger Hospital Centre that I was not in search of my own biological parents and that the names of the patients were of no interest to me, I was provided with a place to work and documents that comprised a 10 per cent sample of persons admitted to the hospital between 1929 and 1939. I would like to express my gratitude to the archivist, Nicole Lacerte, without whom this work would have been impossible.

My research also took me to the Quebec National Archives, where I was able to draw on the photographic resources of Conrad Poirier, and to the Canadian National Archives, where I was once again able to appreciate the efficiency and helpfulness of the archivists in the Manuscript Division and in Documentary Art and Photography. I also consulted newspapers, both in the Bibliothèque nationale du Québec in Montreal and in the National Library in Ottawa. Finally, thanks to the staff at the Fraser-Hickson Institute in Montreal, I was able to lay my hands on certain works that had been almost impossible to find.

How can I express my gratitude to all my colleagues, friends, and students who talked with me about the problems that arose during the composition of this work, who read sections of it, or who simply listened to me and encouraged me? Odette Vincent-Doumey read the manuscript in its entirety and was full of invaluable advice. Those errors that may remain in the final version are, of course, my own. In addition, Jane Lewis supplied me with some useful suggestions for the chapter on unwed mothers. Geoffrey Ewen brought pertinent articles to my attention on a number of occasions. I must mention as well the research associates of the Simone de Beauvoir Institute of Concordia University whose criticism was food for thought. Danielle Juteau, a generous friend, helped me broaden the scope of my work in the course of numerous conversations and put me on the track of the work of the French feminist sociologists. I also profited from the advice of members of the Club du Jeudi, who discussed the chapters on the norm, on deviance, and on prostitution.

1

The Norm

Our image of the Québécoises[1] of two generations ago involves a welter of clichés that now may strike us as laughable – they were mothers of huge families, queens of the household, Children of Mary, Ladies of Saint Anne. It is difficult to believe that their whole lives did not unfold according to the composite profile that the authors of that period have left us – a life consisting of a chaste young womanhood spent in pure company followed by a marriage blessed with numerous offspring, each welcomed with thanks to God. What this study proposes is to try to discriminate the individual from the ideal type, to measure the degree of conformity to the overriding norm, and to determine how representative the terms of the dominant discourse and how effective its dictates were during a particular period.

The elite classes amply pronounced themselves on *the* Québécoise and imposed rigid standards of conduct on her. Did those who were in a position to dictate the terms of the debate reflect an entire population? How fully did the population as a whole heed their advice and exhortations? United by a single religion and a common language, inspired by age-old traditions, the women and men of Quebec would appear to have been a homogeneous group, actuated by identical impulses and sharing the same values. But this entire picture belongs to the realm of myth. Quebec and its inhabitants have always been divided first of all by gender and then by social class. Conformity would likewise be a function of class. Women and men, whether from the bourgeoisie or from the lower classes, would be obedient according to their situation. And in every case, departures from the rules would be evident and would involve quite different consequences.

The study of various kinds of behaviour must be preceded by a consideration of the canons regulating the conduct under observation. Thus, we must remark at the outset that what was ordained varied according to what group was the object of concern. The demands that matter to us here are those that were directed at Quebec women during a clearly defined era, the two decades from 1919 to 1939.

No one would claim that the normative discourse is a faithful indication of how people actually behaved. But even if actual behaviour deviated from the established norm, the public discourse on women did not lose its importance in consequence. In its power, it mapped out what was permitted and what would be repressed. In addition, it constructed an ideal of femininity with which every woman laying claim to a legitimate place in the social order would have to align herself.

Following Simone de Beauvoir, we begin with the premise that one is not born a woman but becomes one. One becomes a woman in the sense that one acquires all the trappings of femininity that are created outside the self and developed within it. In both cases, the shaping takes place according to those norms articulated by those who wield moral and social power and their accepted agents of enforcement. It is these arbiters of the norm who elaborate the qualities that define/construct what society recognizes as "woman" at a particular moment in history. Once the female being has been defined by an anatomy linked to its specific function of reproduction, an entire social construction will be elaborated on the basis of this fact. The prescribed standards deal first of all with this biological function and then with every social function connected to it – with motherhood and its duties.

Furthermore, as a consequence of her physiological specificity, "woman" will present moral qualities that will guarantee proper reproductive order, and these moral qualities are linked in particular to her sexuality. A whole range of directives intended to guarantee chastity, premarital virginity, and a monogamous heterosexuality sanctified by marriage will become the object of a normative discourse that is both imposed and broadly accepted. Women will become "woman" by fulfilling social expectations, particularly those centred on maternity, whether actual or potential, and on a sexuality defined in the first instance by the Other and adopted by those who must submit themselves to that definition.

That women themselves adopted behavioural norms established by the Other, in this case by the men who controlled the Church, the law, the state, and medicine, should come as no surprise, since these women wished to survive in a world defined by male power. Nor is there anything surprising in the fact that the enforcement of the regulations and laws resided as much with women as with the men who pronounced those rules. In other societies, it is women who bind the feet of little girls or perform infibulation on them; in Quebec, survival through marriage, motherhood, and sexual conformity was likewise achieved through an acceptance and a collaboration that must not be confused with consent or with power.[2] Our work inevitably comes within the scope of the study of the structures of oppression – the identification of the oppressors and their instruments and, added to this, the experience of certain of the oppressed, those who, intentionally or not, did not collaborate.

We will first of all be concerned with the working-out of the prescribed standards and with their authors. Thereafter, we will study the obverse of the situation we have defined, that is, the rebels and the nonconformists whose rejection of the norm tipped them over into the realm of deviance.

In a society where the relationship between Church and state was very close, where church attendance was very high, regardless of social class, gender, or geographical region, and where a single religion claimed the adherence of an entire population, the Catholic Church emerged as the primary normative agency. Sociologists have labelled it as total: omnipresent in every sector of society, from the parish to the unions to youth groups to health institutions, it encompassed an audience representative of the Quebec whole.[3] It viewed itself as the interpreter of good and evil, of the commandments of God and of the Church, and as arbiter of what behaviour was approved and what was condemned.

Abundant sources existed to diffuse a hegemonic message. The pastoral letters from the bishops, which recapitulated papal encyclicals, inspired parish sermons. Lenten preaching and lectures, often on secular topics, by members of religious orders were reported in the daily papers. As well, the writings of clerical authors who devoted themselves to the composition of essays, instructive works, and even fiction bulked large in Quebec literature of the twenties and thirties and enjoyed a wide distribution by religious institutions.

How to measure the impact of this whole regulative apparatus? Often enough the young men were standing outside the church when the priest took the pulpit, but the majority of the parishioners, a captive audience, heard the Sunday sermon with a more or less inattentive ear. While Jesuit religious pamphleteering was directed to the educated elite, they had a duty also to disseminate the message. One could hardly plead ignorance of religious directives when their observance could be checked so handily in the confessional.

Since the nineteenth century, the doctor had shared with the priest the secrets of the most intimate activities. The historian Jean-Louis Flandrin and the sociologist Michel Foucault have traced how medicine and then psychoanalysis appropriated gender and sexuality. In the same period, in the course of establishing itself as a profession, medicine eliminated the competition of those not certified by the Corporation of Doctors and Physicians.[4] No less than the priests, the physicians were aware of their power.

Articles published in the medical journals were directed toward a limited audience, to be sure, but they extended beyond the pages of scientific publications. The editor-in-chief of *L'Union médicale,* Dr. Albert Le Sage, reprinted a lecture he gave in Venice in 1936, in which he explained fully "the social influence of the medical press." It "spreads culture, shapes and directs opinion," and accomplishes a "hygienic and moral" task. The medical profession, Dr. Le Sage insisted, could lay claim to the highest scientific objectivity: "Its ideal, its instruction, totally disinterested and devoid of political influence, is inspired by an elevated idea which commands the attention of all."[5] Impartially, the physicians expressed in their writings judgements founded as much on their own conscience as on science. From the learned journals, these were incorporated into the advice dispensed in the consulting rooms or during house calls. As Pauline Fréchette-Handfield observed in 1923 in *La Bonne Parole,* doctors, as experts, were coming to supplant traditional sources of information: "Will the family doctor achieve the place in the home that he should have occupied from the beginning? Will a grandmother, a barren aunt, or a prolific neighbour-lady always go behind his back to give advice that interferes with what he seeks to do?"[6] A number of advertisements, by companies ranging from Phillips' Milk of Magnesia to the Metropolitan Insurance Company, claimed the support of the medical profession.[7] The medical presence in the home would translate the message from scientific to popular language in order to decree what had to be done and what should be avoided to maintain mental and physical health.

Skilled medical advice would often be called upon in social and economic areas. A naive faith in medical training rendered doctors qualified to give their verdicts on the art of child-rearing, good housekeeping, education, work, and the political role of women. Consultation, diagnosis, and cure might be applied to the body politic as to the human body. Elevated to the status of expert in a number of areas, doctors at times held important public offices at City Hall or in the Legislative Assembly, where they made up about 10 per cent of the members.[8] Since handing down a practice from father to son tended to determine membership in the profession,[9] many doctors came from prominent Quebec families and were allied to the upper economic classes, something that added only more weight to what they had to say.

The contribution of doctors to the discussion of reproduction and sexuality proved all the more critical as the female body occupied an important position in pathology. Vulnerable while undergoing the trauma of pregnancy, childbirth, and much thereafter, the female body and its particularities provided a favourite ground for gynecologists, psychiatrists, and even those who did not engrave "specialist in female disorders" on their brass plaques.

The doctors of both body and soul did not enjoy an exclusive monopoly over the definition of appropriate female behaviour. A society that attached such high value to tradition reserved a position of particular importance for women as guardians of religious, linguistic, and cultural values, and politicians, intellectuals, academics, and journalists nominated themselves defenders of women. The discourse of the elected representatives of a population, in this case, of men, is by definition public. In the Legislative Assembly, in the Canadian Parliament, and in local bodies, the politician tries to make sure that his speeches are reported and commented on. Election campaigns give the candidates the opportunity to expound on all the topics of the day and there are any number of pretexts allowing them to hold forth on various kinds of female behaviour. During the 1920s and 1930s, the debate of questions like the pasteurization of milk, paid work for women during times of economic crisis, women's suffrage, police corruption, and the prohibition of children under the age of sixteen from attending the movies revealed attitudes about female nature and female duty. Popular pronouncements on these topics are readily available in the press of the period.

Those who established social standards did not always address the general public. Intellectuals and specialists preferred to reach the elite, whose views would percolate downward to the lower social orders. Thus, starting in 1920, the Semaines sociales du Canada began to be held, days of seminars and study on particular themes of "current affairs," like the family, big business, and property. The Jesuit priest Joseph-Papin Archambault was the originator and first president of these meetings and admitted that they were directed toward an "elite audience . . . the elite thinkers of the race," in order ultimately to influence a "vast section of public opinion."[10] These meetings, which occurred almost every year and which were described as "an examination of the national conscience,"[11] were indeed reported and commented on in the papers. In the end, the seminars were published in book form and journalists and men in public life made reference to them for a considerable time thereafter. As evidence of the special mission of women, the Social Weeks each year welcomed women speakers and placed topics on the agenda dealing with the role of women.

Women were not altogether uninvolved in the formulation of the prescriptives directed toward them. If they were by definition excluded from participation in religious and medical discussion, they had their say within well-defined limits as authors of informal talks and articles.

They had their women's pages, their advice columns: "le Courrier de . . .," their *Revue Moderne,* and the more critical, indeed feminist, journals like *La Bonne Parole* of the Fédération nationale Saint-Jean-Baptiste (FNSJB), the Francophone equivalent of the Canadian Council of Women, and *Sphère féminine* of the suffrage group, Alliance pour le vote des femmes du Québec. Some of them even had their own radio programs. Except for what appeared in the daily press, these texts are difficult to uncover and represent a very small percentage of the publication of the day. Like their male counterparts, these women came from the privileged social classes and they spoke to a select audience.

There was, however, a union press that was close to the working class. In order to hear another side of the story, we must also examine the non-Catholic workers' papers, like *Le Monde ouvrier,* the organ of the international unions to which the majority of organized workers belonged, though, it must be recalled, such workers constituted only 12 per cent of non-agricultural labour.[12]

If the discourse is to be valid, it must be both representative and effective. The range of the writing consulted, from articles to novels, from sermons to defence pleas, assures a representativeness of discursive agencies. They speak in the name of their class and their sex and leave no doubt about the national or religious interests they are defending. One can only wonder about how typical they were and about what meaning to give to all that was said – do they provide a mirror or a model, a portrait or a pious wish? The Quebec mother described by the politicians or the priests is more a part of hagiography than universal reality. Will the generalized portrait of the rebel be any closer to the fact?

The voices of those who did not conform are excluded from the public expression. There might be a pretence of speaking in their name, but they were never represented. The discussion "about" these women[13] reflects the commonplaces, the prejudices, the interests, and the biases of those engaging in it. Thus what is known about women who did not conform comes from what is said by the forces of law and order. The officer who describes the prostitute in the arrest warrant leaves us a dim and subjective picture of a "woman, brown hair, rather tall, medium build, 20-25 years old,"[14] nothing more. The nun who sends a "common, coarse" unwed mother on her way passes down a cliché that recapitulates a whole range of behaviour described in those terms by the authorities of the Hôpital de la Miséricorde.[15] We could multiply the examples drawn from the reports of all those involved who describe their charges. The policeman, the public health officer, or the priest define them, but the subjects rarely openly express themselves and often keep their witness of their own experience to themselves. Their past has to be reconstructed from their gestures rather than from their words.

To write the history of women who have no voices of their own will, as Foucault remarks, involve the archeology of knowledge. It must be composed of whatever has been obscured. What Jacques Derrida calls the "essential shadow of the non-stated"[16] cannot be ignored. The most lamentable silence is that of the women who have been described and to whom attitudes and qualities have been attributed in order that a great deal of advice may be lavished on them. They were not absolutely mute, however. They reveal themselves in letters by inmates of the Hôpital de la Miséricorde, in the testimony of madams in the course of police investigations, and in the remarks of aborted women questioned on their deathbeds. These are precious scraps, but they must also be decoded without forgetting the ears for which they were intended. The woman who is addressing a judge uses a language altogether different from that which she would use to her friends. The letters pleading for liberation from an institution must also be treated with caution, but if the complaints are repeated, the actual situation begins to emerge. Their interpretation remains a matter of judgement; each bit of evidence will be weighed, corroborated, and placed in context.

The targets of all these directives expressed themselves less in words than in their lives. This study owes a great deal to the eloquence of certain gestures set down and duly inscribed in the files – the self-inflicted wound of the unwed mother, the attempts of women under arrest to outwit the police, the flowery false names adopted by prostitutes.

Public discourse rarely limits itself to definitions but issues directives and claims a normative status. It claims effectiveness as well – it exhorts and represses. Thus it gives rise to various modes of check and control – the Roman Catholic confessional, surveillance by the forces of law and order, the machinery of law and court, not to speak of social sanction and the greater or lesser degree of marginalization of non-conformists who become "deviants"; all these give some indication of the power of the discourse. But in order to protect itself and society, deviance conceals itself and is concealed.

If the moral dictates are to be effective, they must be public. Since they were so widely disseminated, they are easy to recognize. But transgressions, shameful and reprehensible as they were, were hidden and thus remain difficult to pick up. Whereas the agent promulgating the received position on women was an institution or a recognized individual speaking publicly, the guilty women kept quiet; the "definers of the situation" themselves transmit the image to us. Agents who intervene and interpret thus mediate the words of those women. They are talked "about"; their words and their behaviour are explained; sources manipulated in this way make dealing with the women themselves a very delicate matter. They will comprise the *subject* of the second part of this book. As such, they must have their say and express their own perception of their own reality. As far as possible, we will allow them this space in order to hear their point of view and their experience.

We must repeat, the image presented of the Québécoise and of the rules to which she had to submit corresponds only to an ideal. It more or less adheres to a reality differentiated according to social class, economic circumstance, and urban or rural area. Instances of repression give some idea of how far the dictates reached, but the margin between what punishment was supposed to follow transgression, on the one hand, and actual punishment or tacit tolerance, on the other, varies according to which period and which group we are looking at. It is useful not to lose sight of this space between edict and reality, between theory and practice, a space symptomatic of anxiety, accommodation, and resistance. This margin can only be mapped through a study of actual behaviours, and these can often only be perceived through the social and judicial consequences that ensued from them.

Both discourse and behaviour appear within a precise historical context. These were the troubled years after the First World War, restless years of economic ups and downs that inspired many an apocalyptic note. These were two decades of great economic fluctuation, punctuated by a rural-urban migration and, until 1930, by an emigration to the United States that acted as a safety valve for surplus labour. Quebec was pursuing a course of urbanization and industrialization that demanded the constant adaptation of a moving, changing population.

Quebec had emerged from the Great War bruised by the crisis over conscription but proud nevertheless of its economic contribution to the Allied cause. Instead of being able to enjoy the calm after the storm, the province was swept by the upheavals that rocked all the Western nations in the aftermath of the hostilities. In common with other large Canadian cities, Montreal saw various economic sectors paralysed by strikes – steelworkers, city employees, and police protesting against salary cuts, a rising cost of living, and the threat of unemployment.[17] Work stoppages and public demonstrations, such as those that brought out thousands of people for Labour Day and May Day, would prove powerless to slow a falling economy in a slump that persisted until the middle of the 1920s.

The economic upturn came about as a result of increased investment from the United States and through a wave of industrialization based on the exploitation of energy resources, on the lumber industry, and on pulp and paper, all developing outside of the two major cities of Quebec and Montreal. A revival of exports stimulated manufacturing in the urban areas where unemployment gradually diminished but never wholly disappeared. In 1929, at the height of an economic boom, the unions reported that 7 per cent of their members were unemployed.[18] The roar of the twenties did not sound in everyone's ears.

The crisis of the 1930s first struck export-based industries, then those based on consumption, but finally none were spared except possibly a few mines in northwest Quebec. Economic recovery had to await the Second World War, but even so, this cannot be termed a "return to normal." The crisis accentuated the divisions between social classes and regional disparity; men and women underwent quite different experiences.

The political stability that had persisted until 1936 did not reflect the economic curves of the period. The leadership of the Liberal Party, in the saddle since the end of the nineteenth century, passed from Lomer Gouin to Alexandre Taschereau in 1920 and the latter remained Premier until 1935. After a brief period under Adélard Godbout, Maurice Duplessis and his Union Nationale took power in 1936, but this government continued the same liberal economic policy as its predecessors. Great political debates proceeded in the opposition but it is evident that Liberal longevity expressed a popular consensus. Third parties did emerge during the thirties and the unions continued to demand labour and social reform.

These economic upheavals attacked institutions and morals. Commentators of the period sound quite alarmed as they describe the undermining of values or the fragility of tradition. The family, that basic unit, and the expression of its spirit, "family values," were under siege by outside forces. Premier Alexandre Taschereau, in a lecture entitled "The Influence of Women on Our National Destiny," implored the members of the Fédération nationale Saint-Jean-Baptiste to "See to it that the families of tomorrow are like those of yesterday."[19] Dr. Antoine-Hector Desloges, hygienist and psychiatrist, missed the simplicity of yesteryear: "Family life does not now exist as once it did. We have been too rich, and we must return to the simple life of the past. This is the only way to remedy the situation."[20]

The discourse of the post-war period is marked with nostalgia. Something had been lost. Recent changes had led to the disintegration of an order that had been believed to be less precarious. The fall of the first "victim" of all this change, the family, which Father Archambault called the "cornerstone of society,"[21] would lead to the collapse of the entire social structure. If the home did not hold out, there would go moral values and standards. The great post-war papal encyclical, *Ubi Arcano,* appeared in Advent, 1922. The Pope imputed the decline of moral values in the cities to the war, which had separated parents from children, and particularly deplored the loss of shame and the looseness of women and girls.[22] Following the encyclical, the bishops of Quebec went even further: "Grave dangers threaten the traditional integrity of our morals, and if these abuses continue, it is only too easy to foresee that our religious observances, our family feeling, our society itself, will be subjected to profound and mortal wounds."[23] If the abuses assaulting social morals were not corrected, the bishops warned, the most dire cataclysms lay in wait for the entire society.

It was by no means an accident that the Semaines sociales of 1923 were convened around the theme of the family. The keynote speech by Father Archambault set the tone: there was a "crisis in the family" that would be the cause of "social disorder and modern anarchy."[24] For several days, speakers chewed over the theme of change for the worse, the recent disintegration of the social order, and the lack of authority. In 1927, the Semaines sociales would take up the subject of authority.

The war was responsible for all these evils, or rather, it had been the catalyst that fostered their appearance. It must be noted that the war had not given rise here to the great upheavals witnessed in Europe. Quebec families had not been ripped apart like those in invaded countries. If some fathers had enlisted or been conscripted, very few mothers had engaged in work outside the home during the First World War. The tenor of the discourse was frequently borrowed from France or Italy, where the losses had been enormous, where women, both married and unmarried, had replaced men in the factories, and where families had been physically torn apart. Nevertheless, one global trauma had not spared Quebec – the influenza epidemic left few families unscathed. Even if the experience of the war was far less immediate in Quebec than in Europe, the same confusion was generally expressed in the face of a loss of paternal authority, the weakening of traditional values, and a relaxation of standards of behaviour.

Local conditions also supported Quebec uneasiness. A surplus rural population had swelled the ranks of unskilled urban workers. This transfer of population, for a Church that placed the highest value on the countryside, had to be combatted. Some observed as well that "model families," that is, extremely large ones, tended to grow smaller in the cities.[25] These rapidly expanding cities were attracting immigrants who were being encouraged to settle there by employers and politicians. Montreal in particular was marked by a cosmopolitanism that, because it was visible, was viewed with alarm. According to Father Archambault, this new and foreign population would always "threaten families" and "introduce their shameless morals."[26]

Married women, those staunch defenders of the home, had not deserted their posts in large numbers to feed the war plants. On the other hand, young unmarried women were finding themselves in the job market in ever greater numbers. They were not just servants or factory workers but office workers, saleswomen, and shop assistants, and they were far more numerous and more noticeable than before the war.[27] The stenographer appeared as an emancipated figure and gave rise to deep anxieties on the part of observers who saw in her another sign that the home was being abandoned. They were disturbed not merely by the poorer families whose young people had to work but by middle-class homes being deserted as well. In a conference called by the Montreal Women's Club and reported in the Montreal daily *Le Canada,* Beatrice Forbes-Robertson Halle regretted that the home was no longer the centre of culture it once had been. "There is only one thing done at home these days, aside from sleeping, eating, and dressing, and that is the cooking of meals,"[28] she observed. Here again, we see a nostalgia for domestic pleasures, which were now often being replaced by bridge clubs, youth groups, and, above all, by the movies.

Although memories of the war and the immediate post-war period were beginning to blur, the discourse persisted. The economic depression in turn provoked nostalgia and feelings of anguish. The economist Édouard Montpetit repeated the exaltation of the home and asked the National Congress of Child Welfare of 1931 to work toward the *restoration* of the family and the expansion of its influence. The newspaper *La Presse* went further in an editorial: "When the family is reinforced, the entire structure of the State is consolidated."[29] Examples of these anxious, alarmist texts could be multiplied, texts that, in a period of harsh reality, looked back toward happier times. The bishops sent out their pastoral letters lamenting the loss of a past in which divorce and abortion seemed to have been unknown,[30] and Madame Edmond Brossard, president of the League of Catholic Women, inquired into "The Causes of Moral Decay in the Family."[31]

The economic role of the family was indeed in question during this period. In the collapse that was ravaging the economy, parents could no longer ensure the survival of their children. The extent of unemployment and the farm crisis forced a turn to the state, where private charity or help within the family had previously sufficed. The social function of the state was always under suspicion in Quebec. Henri Bourassa became the standard-bearer of an entire movement, supported by the clergy, when he opposed the Public Assistance Law of 1921. In 1930, the state had to supplement the inadequate resources of families and of municipalities on the brink of bankruptcy and institute direct aid to those without work. There was worry that paternal authority would be undermined by this sort of intervention. It certainly introduced a variety of social agents, investigators, and bureaucrats into family intimacy. The tiniest business transaction, the slightest paid labour, was to become henceforth accountable. The family had to reveal its secrets and was humbled in the process. The commentators of the period were vaguely aware of it, but they never tackled the question head on, probably because it primarily concerned a class to which they ordinarily did not address themselves.

From the pessimistic discourse that persists throughout these decades, we catch the leitmotif of regret for the idyllic past, anxiety when confronted by the new, a feeling of being invaded by change against which protective barricades must be erected, in short, a rejection of the present and a need to re-establish a lost order. Paternal authority, family feeling, traditional roles – in a word, family stability – were either lost or endangered. Thus, woman, her soul, her inspiration, was called the keystone of the family and of society. The discourse of which she was the object would become disproportionately weighty by reason of these qualities, since her privileged position in an institution so fundamental from a religious as much as a national point of view would inspire a plethora of descriptive and, especially, prescriptive texts.

2

Motherhood

The Normative Discourse

The mother, who stands never so tall as when she is kneeling beside the cradle, in this role deserves a greater solicitude and a greater degree of sympathy from one and all. – *Athanase David,* 1922[1]

The greatest happiness you will ever experience comes each time it is your lot to bring into being the flesh of your flesh. – *Helen MacMurchy,* 1923[2]

Often enough, a woman is a martyr as she brings children into the world. – *E. Manisse,* 1935[3]

How are we to read these quotations? Do they represent contradictory pronouncements, wishful thinking, or popular belief? All three of these commentators, the secretary of the province of Quebec, a physician specializing in the care of children and women, and a priest who preached retreats for young women, share the same perception. The exaltation of motherhood was a recurrent theme along with the possibility of martyrdom as a coveted reward to compensate for the sacrifices that may be demanded. Who then would wish to avoid the honour of consecrating herself to the noble duty of maternity, a duty not confined to the bearing of as many babies as possible but one that required a broad range of maternal qualities if it was to be performed appropriately?

The Official Discourse

Whether she was being described by priest, doctor, or politician, the mother was primarily a figure of love and self-sacrifice. Consider the Lenten meetings held for the Montreal elite: in 1925, Canon Stéphane Coubé attracted crowds to St. Sulpice Hall where he paid homage to the inexhaustible depths of the female heart, formed to suffer and to love. Her heart, proclaimed Canon Coubé, allowed her to dominate the world. No matter who the woman was, once a mother, she was sanctified by that revered vocation, maternity.[4] The following year, Father Audouin poured out his own heart on the subject of feminine qualities – kindness, forbearance, compassion, gentleness, and suffering.[5] It is not necessary to check out each and every Lenten meeting of the period to be convinced that here we have a perennial message. Speaking to their exclusively female audience, since the faithful were segregated according to sex, the male preachers reminded women about their feminine "nature" and the duties deriving from it. Such sermons enjoyed enormous popularity – Notre Dame Church was filled to overflowing; additional space had to be added in St. Sulpice Hall; well-known personalities, judges and doctors, presented and thanked the famous orators, many of whom came from abroad, and what they preached was reported in the newspapers and commented on in the editorial columns. The message was, therefore, fully disseminated.

There was nothing surprising in all this for the women who received the same admonitions from everyone who pronounced a verdict on what woman was and what she ought to be. But were these qualities innate or were they acquired? "Maternal instinct" was invoked so frequently that the qualities associated with it seemed to be innate as well. As Henriette Dessaulles Saint-Jacques, a journalist who wrote in *Le Devoir* as "Fadette," said: "That admirable maternal instinct renders a woman naturally inclined to love her child . . . even among the crudest women, we find that infallible instinct which watches over and preserves humanity."[6] Even so, if the fragile nature of this instinct were admitted, then women had to take care to cultivate those virtues that were, in the long run, in danger of being eroded. It was not only the doctors and confessors who counselled patience and selflessness; so popular a forum as the daily column by "Colette" (Édouardine Lesage) in *La Presse* urged a spirit of sacrifice, acceptance, and resignation for the generations of women readers who wrote for advice.[7] These qualities were associated with those who were destined for motherhood, but they required upkeep and practice, sometimes at heroic cost.

What about women who, although born for motherhood, were forced to deny their vocation? Whether they remained single or entered religious orders, they were supposed to practise an ideal, if not a biological, motherhood. They were to mother their parents, other women's children, or society itself. The headmistress of a high school wrote, "As Monsignor Dupanloup has said, to be fathers is not enough; we must be mothers. How much stronger a reason do we, as nuns, have to be mothers! . . . but we must be worthy, firm, strong, and angelic mothers."[8] More explicitly, Marie Gérin-Lajoie, founder of the Soeurs

AVRIL 1925   MONTREAL, CANADA   6e ANNEE, No. 6

LA REVUE MODERNE

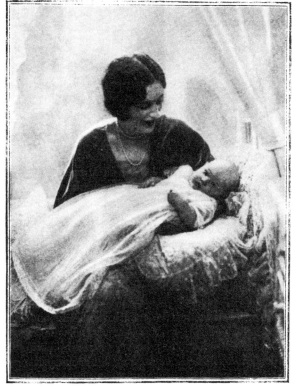

AMOUR MATERNEL

REVUE MENSUELLE   PRIX: 25 SOUS

Maternity was revered and idealized in the official discourse during the interwar period in Quebec. *La Revue moderne* (avril 1925).

du Bon-Conseil, recognized that women were not always destined to set up a household. Those women who would choose a celibate religious life were entrusted by the Church with "a great number of particularly maternal tasks, such as the education of children, care of the sick, and aid to the poor."[9] Nuns, especially teachers and nurses, should have had no difficulty seeing themselves accepted as substitute mothers. Nor did they have any doubts about the value of their way of life. Father Victorin Germain, who was deeply concerned with the moral problems of his era, especially with sexual morality, frankly posed the question: "Is the mother of a family superior to the nun?" and answered it: "The state or vocation of mother remains inferior to the religious vocation or profession; but the faithful called to the one as to the other vocation may attain the highest degree of sanctity."[10] Thus reassured, mother or nun might swell the ranks of sainthood by wielding her maternal qualities in her own sphere.

Unmarried women who took care of their relatives, taught school, or were servants in the parish rectory enjoyed an uncertain social status. One can also turn to folksongs and popular expressions, like "being on the shelf," for images of unmarried women that present them as bordering on the ridiculous. Nevertheless, one woman in eight would never marry.[11] Without a man to support her, a woman generally led a life of servitude but did not abandon those "natural" qualities that could not find appropriate expression. Deprived of objects on which to lavish their maternal virtues, spinsters preserved the instinct to set their hearts on something or other, if only a domestic animal. The author Henriette Tassé wrote: "We ought never ridicule the old maid who dotes on a dog or a cat; it is her maternal instinct which cannot find the right road."[12] Before we laugh, we must understand the importance the author attributed to this instinct. A few years later she would affirm: "Maternal energy is the force through which selflessness and industry came into the world."[13]

Might we conclude that without motherhood, woman was nothing? A reading of the fiction of the period might lead us to that conclusion. Janine Broynard-Frot has analysed novels rooted in Quebec and concluded that the ultimate destination of women was indeed procreation: "Once she had fulfilled this role, she was free to leave the scene."[14] The single woman married, became a mother, and her story was over. In her study of "the emergence of the feminine in the literary tradition of Quebec,"[15] Patricia Smart concludes that "the real mother, corporeal, human, and loving, is absent [from these works], killed . . . by the Father who is simultaneously frightened by the power of women to give birth and who holds them prisoner in their reproductive role."[16] The story of a woman with such a destiny would have little dramatic interest.

Woman is defined by maternity; given its essential qualities, it would be against nature for her to deviate from its course. Paradoxically, however, the entire educational apparatus was devoted to incubating and orienting her nature. Her first dolls were there to be cuddled, dressed, fed, and, of course, loved. With the advent of puberty, the lesson became more pointed. According to Dr. L.P. Mercier, "It is at this point that the girl must begin to realize that, by reason of her physical and moral qualities, her entire life is headed for the one great aim of motherhood."[17] The mother was charged with preparing her daughter, first by her example and then by judicious counsel. "Fadette," for whom the maternal instinct was indestructible, conceives the mother as shaping and engraving her children's minds. She advises her middle-class sisters not to leave this education entirely to the nanny, who is there merely to lend a hand. The school was likewise charged with educating girls with an eye out for their future mission.[18]

Prepared and equipped, the woman was qualified for those physical and social functions for which her biology and education had destined her. It was for the modern young woman of the post-war period, rather than for her parents, to choose the best person to assure a harmonious marriage – a sober, protective husband who would properly administer the material goods of the wife, reduced by marriage to the status of a minor; who would share his paternal authority with her and allow her to reign in the home. Some would even require a eugenic marriage, free of hereditary taints that might compromise the future of the race. Once the selection was made, marriage would provide the physical framework for motherhood, which, with the coming of the child, became the basis of the family. For, from the earliest centuries of the Christian era, the purpose of marriage was first and foremost to have children and then, in second place, to relieve the sexual urges of the husband.[19]

Thus, for the Church, motherhood was more than a natural function, an assumed duty; it was the mission that legitimated the sexual union of the couple as well. If the aim of the common life of the married couple is reproduction, nothing should stand in its way and everything should tend to foster it. In 1930, the encyclical *Casti Connubii* reiterated Rome's objections to birth control. The statement only reinforced the directives of the clergy, who, well before the papal letter, lost no opportunity to remind couples of their duty to reproduce. The priests took upon themselves the duty of combatting the "homicidal habits" to which married couples, especially in the cities and urban centres, appeared to be devoted.[20] At the Semaine sociale of 1923, Father Olivier Maurault identified the two great menaces to the family: "whatever interferes with creation and whatever hinders the education of children." He blamed the publicity given to "deplorable practices," because "there is only one means of limiting a family, *when there is a grave reason to do so,* and that is *continence.*"[21] On the same occasion, Father Henri Martin saw the abandonment of the countryside as one of the numerous causes of the fall in the birth rate. He pointed out the marked difference between rural and urban fertility rates and wondered whether the scourge of French Malthusianism[22] also lay in wait for Quebec. According to the text presented by Father Martin to this natalist conference, vice had already crept in, propagated by intemperance, divorce, the masculinization and egotism of women, the dances and sports to which young people were devoted, too-small lodgings, and even by honeymoons, "a deplorable custom which renders so many marriages sterile and women valetudinarian."[23]

The clergy went so far as to seek support from medical science, as if the religious arguments needed bolstering by material proof. Priests and physicians supported one another in their natalist arguments. Father Martin asked doctors to reassure women and inform them about what the celebrated French apostle of scientific baby-care, Adolphe Pinard, affirmed – that a woman does not achieve her completion until the third child.[24] In a 1936 work on heredity, a Trappist monk declared, "It is a fact attested to by every conscientious physician that a woman experiences physiological ailments which are all the more serious when she habitually indulges in contraceptive practices – those few rare children which she does have will be lacking in physical resistance," and from this he deduced that the last-born child of a large family would often be the most vigorous.[25] But even large families might be planned. To allow for this, the Church sanctioned the Ogino-Knauss method. In his manual on sexuality, Father Germain found it, under certain circumstances, to be "a legitimate means of spacing births."[26] In any event, a prior consultation with the confessor was required to establish the legitimacy of the reasons for resorting to the rhythm method.

A number of Quebec doctors publicly declared themselves opposed to any artificial contraceptive procedure. Dr. Gaston Lapierre could find only "an egotistical and exaggerated individualism" in summing up the disastrous consequences of contraception: "More and more neuropathic women, premature ageing, uterine fibroids, certain organic scleroses, complete neurasthenia, nervous imbalances, uterine cancer caused by more than one chemical irritant used habitually."[27] At the time of the trial of Dorothea Palmer in Eastview (now Vanier), a suburb of Ottawa, who was accused of distributing information and contraceptive devices, Dr. Léon Gérin-Lajoie, professor of obstetrics at the University of Montreal, testified against the use of mechanical means of interfering with fertilization, as he considered it to be harmful.[28]

To reach complete fulfilment, the woman had to give birth. *La Mère canadienne et son enfant,* a manual published by the Child Welfare Division of the Department of Health in Ottawa and distributed without charge in dispensaries and doctors' offices, begins, in the first sentence of the first chapter, with these words: "Motherhood is the realization of woman's ultimate destiny and marks the full blossoming of her existence."[29] Pregnancy, under the care of a professional, should bloom often and unimpeded.

Completion was conferred by maternity. This female blossoming would become more than an individual objective; it would act as the realization of a collective destiny and play a primordial role in the nationalist designs of the period. In 1918, the Jesuit priest Louis Lalande printed the text of a speech he had delivered on "The Revenge of the Cradle" in the journal, *L'Action française.* To understand "how to achieve this revenge," he recommended observing "the young French-Canadian mother lifting the child of the previous year from his cradle and teaching him his first lesson in sacrifice: 'Give up your bed, my darling, to your little brother who has just arrived; he will give it to a little sister next year.'"[30] Father Archambault proclaimed: "This primacy of fertility, to which is linked our ethnic survival, must be maintained at any cost . . . ."[31]

Such encouragement to prolific child-bearing squares very well with the social context of Quebec in the twenties and thirties, decades marked by a proliferation of nationalist groups. It was deemed necessary to increase the numbers and protect the racial and religious homogeneity of Quebec society. In 1933, "Fadette" praised the manifesto of the most recent nationalist organization, Jeune Canada. The organizational statement was addressed to agricultural and professional youth, but ignored young women. Therefore, the columnist attempted to repair the deficiency: "My dear young friends, remain with us, in our world. . . . Maintain cordial relationships with the English, but never let them pass into intimacy. . . . It is always the French family that becomes English, and Protestant too, in short order."[32] The "revenge of the cradle," survival, the depopulation of the countryside, colonization, immigration, and demographic projections were all fodder for passionate debate. The losses experienced in the Great War had made the West aware of the importance of numbers and the need to replace those who had fallen. The migration of people from the country to the city, to an environment less favourable to large families, stimulated anxiety about the loss of rural values and numerous offspring. Immigration from Europe, especially from Britain, threatened ethnic balance and provoked appeals for prolific reproduction. The changes taking place in the composition of the population inspired fears to which no one was immune.

The figures do not support these anxieties. In 1919, 80,081 babies were born in Quebec, representing 34 per cent of births in Canada. Ten years later there were 81,380 (34 per cent), and at the outbreak of World War Two, 76,621 (34.6 per cent). For the same period, the population of Quebec went from 26.8 per cent to 28.9 per cent of the Canadian whole.[33] If Quebec was producing 6-8 per cent more births than might be expected of its population in relation to the rest of Canada, emigration explains its diminished demographic importance in the Canadian scene. In this regard, we can hear the values of the priests and physicians echoed in the pronouncements of politicians. The Liberal minister Athanase David never stopped talking about the "sacred calling of the French-Canadian mother.... We shall know how to pay attention to the cradle where she will have laid her child, in order to make of this child a man, who will in time be an asset to his homeland."[34] Every occasion served as a pretext to render non-partisan, unanimous homage to the women who had contributed to populating Quebec. In a speech in honour of Deputy J.O. Renaud, father of sixteen, the deputy conservator, Arthur Sauvé, proclaimed that "the health of the province resided in its large families."[35] For the nationalists, who were clericals in addition, praise of the mother and disquiet at the loss of French-Canadian strength to the United States became ever more pressing.

We must not assume that this discussion of the primary function of women was exclusive to Quebec. We come across it in 1918 in the House of Commons, as women were granted the right to vote in federal elections, and in the following year, with the creation of the Department of Health. It was repeated as well in Ontario by those decrying emigration to the United States and by the nativists who saw Anglo-Saxon Canada threatened by European immigration. Outside of Quebec, however, it never achieved the same level of urgency. On the other hand, one will search almost in vain for dissenting Francophone opinion. There were no neo-Malthusians or birth control clinics in Quebec. In 1932, however, the author Henriette Tassé adopted a eugenicist position and called for contraception to improve the quality of the race and, as a practical measure, to prevent abortion and reduce the incidence of prostitution. Compared to other spokespersons of her era, she appears as an iconoclastic figure when she holds that many moral edicts have become outdated or are even injurious. She never expressed such ideas publicly, however, and if other women concurred with her, they also remained silent.[36]

The interest in women's reproductive role was not limited to reproduction as such but extended to everything related to child care. The first duty of the mother was to nourish her child. For several generations there had been a choice: breast or bottle. This was not a question to be decided solely on the grounds of health – the Church had made

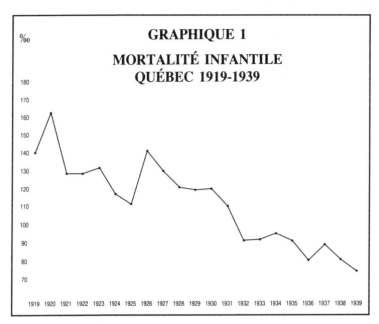

‰

GRAPHIQUE 1

MORTALITÉ INFANTILE QUÉBEC 1919-1939

Figure 1. Infant Mortality, Quebec, 1919-1939
SOURCE: Québec, Rapport Annuel du Service provincial d'hygiène.

maternal feeding a moral duty, as the preachers did not fail to remind the faithful. Father Audouin, in a lecture at Notre Dame Church entitled "Mother and Child," reminded women that they had a duty to breast-feed unless the doctor prescribed otherwise.[37] More and more women were choosing the bottle, which was not without consequences for the health of the newborn. If the milk was pasteurized and kept in an icebox or, in middle-class households only, in a refrigerator, and if the bottles and nipples were properly sterilized, the baby would probably come to no harm. In the case of powdered formulas, these were to be mixed with water that had to be boiled as a precaution. If, however, as was common just after the war, the milk was not pasteurized, was diluted if not dirty, and if the only way of keeping it fresh was to run cold water from the faucet over the bottle, the danger of a gastro-intestinal infection was only too real.[38] Health officials were very disturbed by the alarming rate of infant mortality in Quebec, hence their concern with breast-feeding. The link between infant mortality and "artificial" forms of feeding made breast-feeding a patriotic duty.[39]

Even when the unhealthiness of cow's milk was not an issue, women who had renounced a function dictated by their biology continued to be scolded for their selfishness. Arguments based on nature

Faites profiter votre bébé du bénéfice inestimable de l'alaitement maternel. Vous en suivrez les progrès marqués — ceux que reconnaissent les plus célèbres autorités médicales qui déclarent qu'aucune nourriture ne peut égaler pour l'enfant le lait maternel, parce qu'il est un aliment parfait, exempt de tout germe, une sauvegarde contre les maladies causées par une mauvaise nutrition, le rachitisme par exemple.

"*Ne SAURIEZ-vous pas que je suis Allaité?*"

OVALTINE
ALIMENT — TONIQUE — LIQUIDE

Permet aux mères d'allaiter leurs bébés.

Ovaltine advertisement. From *La Revue moderne* (mai 1932).

always carry a lot of weight. Adopting artificial feeding, like every offense against nature, would incur dire consequences. Dr. Lapierre observed that breast-feeding added to feminine beauty, but those women who shirked their duty ran the risk of swelling the ranks of women who fade before their time. He repeated Dr. Pinard's warning: "A uterine tumour lies in wait for every woman who has not breast-fed by the age of 25."[40] Dr. Joseph Gauvreau, Registrar of the College of Physicians and Surgeons and one of the founders of *l'Action française*, left no doubt about the sacrifices expected of the mother; even if breast-feeding was a kind of slavery because, he believed, the breast-feeding mother must continually deprive herself, he condemned those mothers who are "guilty of going on a feeding-strike."[41] Not until the end of the 1930s, when refrigeration was widespread and the battle against contaminated milk was almost won, do we find a pediatrician approving of bottle-feeding. Dr. Daniel Longpré of Notre Dame Hospital, a modern doctor, cited his American colleagues who were advocating a more verifiably scientific form of feeding. He argued that most women, though willing, were unable to continue breast-feeding for a very long time; thus it was advisable to pay attention to a balanced diet and the purity of the food.[42] In any event, it would be up to the doctor to decide.

Whether it was to be breast or bottle, the mother had the prime responsibility, but she now would be taken in hand by the health experts. In this life-or-death decision, instinct was not enough. The mother would be overseen and advised by the now-indispensable physician. Dr. J.A. Beaudoin, in his *Cours d'hygiène,* and his colleague, Dr. Gaston Lapierre, in his baby-care manual, stressed the importance of medical attention to assure that the pregnancy would go to term and the infant survive.[43] The handbooks of advice to mothers insisted on the necessity of medical control. In *La Mère canadienne et son enfant,* the brief catch phrases at the bottom of each page repeat the same message:

"The doctor's care is the best prevention against illness."

"Ask someone who knows – the doctor."

"If you are at all unwell, consult your doctor."

"Assure the health of your child – have the doctor check him over."[44]

Neither pregnancy, nor childbirth, nor child care could be left in women's hands. Midwives had long since been declared incompetent;[45] close relatives, who used to follow the developing pregnancy, were deemed ignorant of the advances in child care; finally, the mother herself, who had to tend to the survival and health of her own child, often guided by her own mother's advice, was also seen to be incapable of doing so without the advice of specialists.

The mother, as both responsible and incompetent, was duty-bound to repair her deficiencies. When Dr. Beaudoin listed the causes of infant mortality, he concluded that mothers' ignorance subsumed all the others.[46] It was only a small step from there to the suggestion that, in their negligence, mothers might be murderers. According to Dr. Joseph Gauvreau, newborns who perished died because they were without a mother, even if she were still alive and at home, because she was not a mother "if, by reason of intelligence, neglect, or ignorance, she did not fulfil the role that God and nature had assigned her."[47] The statistics were there to demonstrate that babies who did not receive a doctor's care were at greater risk than those who regularly attended the clinics. In 1925, a study by the Child Welfare Association showed that 75 per cent of babies who died had never been brought to a public health clinic.[48] The mother, in whom no one had a great deal of confidence, had to depend on the services of professionals if she were to accomplish her "mission."

Mothers who started out as parents and caretakers had to become educators as well. They could not lightly dissociate themselves from this task. Mothers who did poorly at it would create a load of social and moral problems. Above everything else, they were responsible for their children's moral training and for their daughters' sexual education. They were to protect their daughters against fashion, dance, and every other occasion of sin for which they were ultimately accountable. After all, as Monsignor Georges Gauthier, Coadjutor Archbishop of Montreal, pointed out, "They are the most certain architects of the spiritual ruin of their children."[49]

The responsibility for the physical and moral health of their offspring involved a large number of domestic duties for Catholic mothers. As guardians of Quebec culture and tradition, they had to preserve and transmit this heritage to the next generation while shielding it from the innovations and temptations of modern life. During Lent in 1926, Father Audouin enumerated the burdens of the wife-mother. As his list is more or less representative of the standards demanded in the period, it is worth pausing a moment over the obligations charged to women as mothers. Of course, they were to "remain in the home," their "realm," and do so without being lazy, flighty, or frivolous. They were to manifest all the tenderness necessary to "humanize" their husbands and minister to "their broken bodies and their weary souls," and prevent them from being swallowed up by drink. Sisters of charity that they were, they would know how to pardon those who "remained children all their lives."[50] Trained to mother their children, they were to apply the same techniques to their husbands.

Roles

In the same period a woman, Mme. Louis Coderre, a member of the FNSJB, took a similar line. In a lecture on the home, Mme. Coderre reiterated the elements of woman's role, "by reason of her natural talents," as "steward, educator, and dispenser of all manner of good." Within the family, order, economy, and religion constituted her triple responsibility, a responsibility that had repercussions throughout society as a whole. "A society is worth only as much as the family." An enormous moral power was thus invested in the wife and mother who guaranteed "the health or corruption of society, according to whether families are sound or corrupted."[51] All the pundits of the period had faith in this power, at least among those who may be called the social elite.

Armed with the virtues of self-denial, devotion, and selflessness so necessary to their role as mothers, women were by extension to assume those obligations linked more or less closely to their motherhood – they were to become educators, caregivers, psychologists, and book-keepers. These functions required the continued presence of the mother among her children. Society must not shrink from taking any measure to prevent her from yielding to the temptation to leave the home and its duties. Some ten years after Mme. Coderre's pronounce-ments, Sister Marie Gérin-Lajoie, who was very active in the FNSJB, presented almost the same views once again and outlined an entire pro-gram to encourage women to remain in the home: family allowances, home relief so that the mother need not work outside the home, a return to the countryside, better organized domestic help, family education, fairer legislation for married women. "The situation which she will fill the best"[52] is as guardian of the household, where the wife might enjoy the fullest flowering of her highest faculties.

In this post, regardless of the extent of her powers, she remained subordinate to her husband, whose position was confirmed by both religion and law. According to Leo XIII, in his encyclical *Arcanum Divinae Sapientiae* (1880), "the husband is the authority in the family and the head of his wife."[53] In the organic vision of the family expressed by the Church and the Civil Code, the parents ought to exer-cise their authority jointly, but in cases where they disagreed the father's will was to prevail.[54] Despite all the maternal responsibility for the children's education, only the father's consent was required for a minor to marry. The view of the family as a hierarchical structure dominated by the father was so important that it provided an argument against communism, that great terror of the 1930s. A 1932 brochure from the École sociale populaire, an apostolic social mission directed by the Jesuits, castigated "anti-family communism" for four reasons, all of which were linked to the threat it posed to the traditional family. The condemnation of communism must be unrelenting because "its doctrine of perfect equality between the rights of the head and those of the members destroys the hierarchy of the family and lays ruin to pater-nal authority."[55] This patriarchal discourse is not just a stale, isolated whiff of the nineteenth century; we come across it in 1940 in the writ-ings of the Oblate Father Turcotte, who reaffirms the notion that "the wife is not the equal of the man in the family, where, by the grace of God, he is both head and king."[56]

Even the "maternal feminists" writing in *La Bonne Parole* accepted this division of roles: the man is "the minister of external affairs," the wife "the minister of the interior"; "while he goes out about his busi-ness, his wife is busy about the house."[57] The impenetrable quality of feminine and masculine roles rested on the essential difference between the attributes of the two sexes as created by Divine will. In the home, as in the harmonious beehive, a frequently recurring image, each had his or her own well-defined tasks, none of which was interchangeable. Stability, "the Christian social order," depended on this division. The husband was to watch over his wife and protect and support her, educate her to the demands of serious life, provide the material necessities, and assist her as mother.[58] *Le Livre des mères canadiennes,* by Dr. Helen MacMurchy of the Child Welfare Division of the Department of Health in Ottawa, mentions several other paternal duties: he should make breakfast to help his pregnant wife deal with her morning sickness, register the birth of the newborn "to prove he is a Canadian and a British subject," and act as a model to his baby who will imitate him.[59] Canon Louis-Adolphe Paquet, philosopher, educator, and dean of the faculty of theology at the University of Laval, must have been aware that fathers had other things to do besides educating their children, for while he decreed that "the father ought to bring all his resources and advice to bear on the education of his children," he added, "but as he is often absent, sometimes for weeks at a time, maternal involvement is indispensable."[60] The wife might inherit those responsibilities delegated to her by her husband, but in no way would paternal authority be diluted.

As the children grew, domestic responsibilities became less pressing. Then only could the mother make the most of her virtues and exercise her ministry outside the confines of her home. Freed from caring for her children, who were being looked after by a maid or who had flown the nest, she should be able to allow herself to try to apply her talents to the improvement and cleansing of her surroundings. The idealized image of the Québécoise mother should logically have led to her adopting a heavy burden of social and political responsibilities. But, although she was morally superior, free from all material and personal considerations, and imbued with altruism, she was to limit her field of endeavour to the immediate welfare of her family in what may usefully be called the private sphere.

To confirm this separation between the public and private spheres, the great maternal qualities were invoked. That they were embedded in nature and in Divine intention was reiterated in the teachings of both the Church and medicine. Catholic thinkers founded this functional split on nature and on the Pauline tradition of the subjection of women, as repeated by Thomas Aquinas, to remind women that their moral superiority, far from destining them to public influence, must be confined to the home or, at a pinch, to philanthropy.

The religious discussion of the public role of women in Quebec cannot be undertaken without reference to Monsignor L.-A. Paquet. His prestige in educational circles came from his philosophy textbook, his writings on the education of girls, and his campaign for domestic science education. Just after the First World War, in two articles forcefully attacking feminism, he developed a theory of the difference between masculine and feminine function based on physical difference and, by extension, the moral qualities pertaining to each sex. He took aim at egalitarian feminism and particularly at those feminists who demanded "the reform of marriage and the domestic emancipation of the wife." This feminism is only "a perverse movement, a false ambition which drags the most elegant half of our species out of its proper path and threatens the basis of both family and society."[61] The man must preside as head of the household in which the wife will remain confined because of "her very sex, in which the most generous instincts of our nature vibrate, and where loving gentleness and pacifying goodness are enshrined, far from the quarrels of the public forum and the tumult of the public arena."[62] Monsignor Paquet exercised a strong influence but, if he was one of the most eloquent of opponents, he was not the only religious figure to attack feminism. In 1920, in the course of a discussion of the "duties of the wife and mother," Cardinal Bégin condemned feminist doctrines that would turn the wife away from her proper duties to "toss her into the public arena and make her a rival of the man."[63] Once again, nature, the essential feminine linked to motherhood, is made to shoulder the weight of religious prescriptives as applied to politics.

Even if Canon Paquet and his imitators wanted to shield women from political life, more and more social agencies were attempting to recruit benevolent and charitable citizens. The tradition of public service had long been established among English Canadians and was gradually putting down roots among Francophones, even if in Quebec the religious communities had rendered lay service less of a necessity. On the condition that they did not neglect their family responsibilities, the more educated and less economically dependent women of the middle class could turn toward social reform.

Motivated in the first instance by the desire to do good to others, they could devote themselves to social work. For middle-class women, like the members of the FNSJB, charitable works were simply an extension of their domestic concerns and called for similar qualities of devotion and self-sacrifice. For Alphonse Désilets, head of the provincial domestic science service and member of the board of the provincial School of Domestic Science, "it is a well-known psychological fact that the strongest motive for action among women is the desire to do good to others."[64] According to Henriette Tassé, if world peace should one day come about, it would be because of women, "who being more aware of human life, will have united around the world to end all war."[65] Feminism was to be maternal first of all and its demands were to be made in the name of charity rather than of justice.

Educators, doctors, priests, politicians, and the feminists of the FNSJB all urged that structures be erected to foster the implementation of the discourse concerning motherhood. From sermons at feminist conferences to medical treatises to scholarly articles, the message was uniform: the woman was to be a mother above everything else; motherhood must flourish unrestrained in the family, which was united by the indissoluble bonds of matrimony.

It is hard to exaggerate the image of the Québécoise as the social thinkers of the era would have desired to construct it. Searching for dissenting opinion, the only discordant note is struck in the labour and Communist press. In *Le Monde ouvrier,* the journal of the international unions, Julien Saint-Michel wrote on several occasions about feminism, women's education, and women's work. These columns appear to be the product of an enlightened male consciousness, but in fact the masculine pseudonym hid the identity of Eva Circé-Côté, writer, poet, librarian, and founder of the Montreal municipal library. Few then or now were aware of her identity as a columnist in the labour press. The modern women she describes is certainly a less idealized figure. She has not been created solely for maternity and thus has the right to an education equal to her brothers. This journalist even took on the Lenten preacher of 1925, Canon Coubé, for the image of women he had presented at Saint Sulpice.[66] In Quebec the international unions, while not atheist, kept their distance from the clergy and from the nationalist intellectuals. The opinions expressed in their publications were not, however, uniformly progressive. As unemployment raged during the Great Depression, the journalist R. Hachette and even Gustave Francq, the editor of *Le Monde ouvrier* and secretary of the Trades and Labour Congress of Canada (TLC), returned to the theme of the "natural role" of women at home, taking care of the children.[67] Actually, in 1931, only 2.88 per cent of Quebec married women older than fifteen claimed to be in paid employment.[68] Economic considerations underlay these maternalist positions, which were not always shared by Saint-Michel. Nevertheless, the influence of the international unions never extended beyond a narrow group in the population; the TLC had just 35,000 members in Quebec in 1929.

The Communist papers, *Vie ouvrière,*[69] *L'Ouvrier canadien* in 1930 and 1931, and *Clarté* offered an image of women primarily as workers and emancipated, but from a perspective that did not depart all that far from maternalist ideology. The wife of a Communist worker did not necessarily have a job of her own but played a secondary role, supporting workers' strikes and teaching proletarian values to her children.

An advertisement for a sanitarium run by the Good Shepherd Sisters for women suffering from nervous complaints, alcoholism, and drug addiction. From *La Revue moderne* (novembre 1924).

It is hardly surprising that groups far removed from the centres of religious and political power should present dissenting views on the appropriate role of women in society. The modernity of their arguments stands out in sharp contrast to the official positions mired in tradition. Their position on the role of women was perceived more as a threat than as a viable option. The positions taken by the unions and the left in no way weakened the power of the dominant discourse and the policies it inspired.

Normative Practices

This insistence on the essential difference between the attributes and respective functions of each sex did not remain in the ideal realm of speculation and theory. Laws, institutions, and practices enshrined the prescribed definition of maternal qualities and obligations that flowed from the discourse, establishing limitations on behaviour and deterring transgression.

Exactly like the Church, the law came to define the context for motherhood: the married pair. The indissolubility of marriage was the cement that held the institution of the new family firmly in place. The Civil Code in force in Quebec made divorce difficult and costly but the federal Parliament could occasionally dissolve a marriage contracted by two Quebec residents. This federal power met with frequent opposition in Quebec. The intransigent Henri Bourassa demanded the abolition of the power of the Senate in matters of divorce as well as the suppression of every divorce tribunal in the country. He based his arguments on both morality and provincial jurisdiction.[70] The necessity to seek a private member's bill in Ottawa surely discouraged many who had to be content with a legal separation, in itself something of a disgrace. The separation from bed and board, the final recourse of couples in distress, raised the question of the wife's financial security. Yet again, nothing would be allowed to encourage the break-up of the family. In 1923, Judge Bruneau announced his opposition to overly generous support payments, which only acted as "bait for a large number of women" and increased the number of separations.[71] Marriage breakdown was condemned not only because of the position of the Roman Catholic Church but also, as the Semaine sociale of 1923 repeated, because it led to the "disruption of families" and was the direct cause of depopulation, a spectre forever haunting the Quebec elite classes.[72]

That the Quebec Civil Code restricted access to divorce in the province did not prevent Quebec members of Parliament from expressing themselves on federal bills concerning divorce. Every time divorce came up for debate, the members from Quebec took the opportunity to attack it. In 1925, Parliament discussed equalizing the grounds for divorce in order to make adultery uniformly serious for both parties. Francophone MPs and senators came to the defence of the indissolubility of marriage. They all invoked nature, tradition, and Catholic doctrine, but MP Thomas Vien and Senator Thomas Chapais also warned against the disastrous consequences of divorce on the birth rate.[73] Every time the dissolution of marriage might have been facilitated by a change in legislation, as in 1930 with the establishment of a divorce court in Ontario, the representatives from Quebec linked arms across party lines and presented a common front in opposition.[74]

Divorce, while never very common, was nevertheless always on the increase; in 1930 the figures disturbed the Church to the point that it issued a pastoral letter on the subject.[75] No movement in Quebec supported the liberalization of the divorce laws, and Judge C.E. Dorion's remarks at the Semaine sociale du Canada in 1931 are quite representative: "It is not necessary to provide Catholics with the temptation to seek relief from those real or imaginary evils from which they, like everyone else, may suffer."[76] Exceptionally, one could seek a Vatican annulment on very particular grounds. Engaged couples knew what to expect and knew that they were married for life. The institution remained unalterable, the Church inflexible, and no divorce court would be established in Quebec until 1964.

Opposition to the birth control movement was expressed in the laws forbidding contraception. Under attack by the Church from the twelfth century onward,[77] contraceptive practices had been the subject of laws since the nineteenth century. In 1892, the Canadian Criminal Code made it a criminal offence to sell or advertise products that interfered with conception or were capable of producing an abortion.[78] The law against contraceptives was rarely enforced and condoms and diaphragms could be obtained in certain pharmacies as well as other public places. There was at least one prosecution, in 1938, of a newspaper seller who also peddled condoms on the train from Montreal to Rimouski. When Jack Cherry offered condoms in a box of three for fifty cents in addition to his usual goods, a passenger who turned out to be a policeman did not hesitate to arrest him. Cherry pleaded guilty and was fined \$25.[79] The whole business seems to have been rather unusual and aroused little interest in the newspapers. It is only of interest here because it demonstrates the existence of a law that could be invoked at any opportune moment.

The religious and civil edicts against abortion were considerably more severe. The Church had come out categorically against the practice. Its position on contriving the expulsion of the fetus was clear. In 1869, Pius IX decreed the excommunication of anyone successfully producing an abortion. The status of the woman who submitted to the operation was left undecided. In 1917, the question was resolved by article 2350 of the Code of Canon Law, which included the aborting female among those subject to excommunication by a bishop.[80] The question of conscience and the medical code of ethics arose when the survival of the mother required the termination of her pregnancy. The removal of a viable fetus to save the mother's life was considered "an abortion or simple murder." As a priest of the era explained, "when she marries, a woman must assume the risks inherent in her new condition,"[81] but how many were aware of what they were getting into? In his *Point d'Interrogation,* Father Germain considered it a good idea to refer to articles 303-306 of the Criminal Code as well as ecclesiastical law in order to justify the grave religious sanctions imposed on an act the Church viewed not only as homicide but also as one that consigned the unbaptized fetus to limbo.[82] It would appear that the faithful had to be reminded periodically that these practices were forbidden. In 1939, the *Semaine religieuse de Montréal* was moved to reproduce a passage from a pastoral letter by Monsignor Audollent, the Bishop of Blois, denouncing abortion in his own country.[83] Quebec was not immune from what was seen as an international catastrophe.

Since the nineteenth century, abortion had been not merely a sin but also a crime. In 1861, An Act Concerning Offenses Against the Person made those involved in abortion liable to life imprisonment. Article 303 of the Criminal Code applied to an abortionist of either sex as well as to the aborted woman, whether she was actually pregnant or not and at any time during the pregnancy.[84]

The family that had to be preserved was a hierarchical family, one with the man at its head. This privilege, however, did involve certain legal obligations. Barring a legitimate excuse, the husband was required to provide for his wife and children under sixteen. During the Great Depression, many were unable to live up to their obligations, as cases before the courts during the thirties attest. In 1934, *La Presse* reported a virtual epidemic as twenty-four heads of families appeared in court on a single February morning.[85] Most of the women who were deserted lacked the means to seek legal redress, but if they required charity or direct family assistance an attempt was made to catch up with the husband to force him to shoulder his responsibilities if he was earning a wage. Welfare organizations also took it upon themselves to locate recalcitrant husbands to bring them to Recorder's Court.[86] In 1931, the Montreal Society for the Protection of Women and Children prided itself on having traced 54 per cent of the "deserters," which made up almost a quarter of all its cases.[87] Women were economically dependent on their husbands both through the force of civil law and by reason of the difficulties experienced by married women who sought work outside the home. Should the husband disappear, the consequences were tragic for his wife and children, who were solely dependent on the father's salary for their support.

The law was there not simply to protect an institution believed to be threatened; it also offered both encouragement and restraints to assure that the normal family, as defined by the elite classes, would be maintained. Family members, especially mothers, had to be provided with the means to carry out their responsibilities.

Since the First World War, the state had concerned itself with the lot of widows and indigent mothers who were wives of soldiers. Following Manitoba's lead, the provinces extended support to all widows and mothers in need. In Quebec, the legislators were reluctant to follow suit until 1937. The question was frequently debated and it will come as no surprise that the nationalists and members of the clergy joined their voices to those of the women's groups that called for widows' pensions and payments to mothers who were supporting their families. The FNSJB wanted to see support payments for single mothers who were raising their children so that they might stay at home and avoid the necessity of working outside and "keep them in their place in charge of their children."[88] Along the same lines, the Montpetit Commission on social affairs used moral arguments to bolster its recommendation for support payments to mothers in need. As the report states, "The witnesses are in agreement in stating that the presence of children in the home is an effective moral protection for needy mothers."[89] Since the nineteenth century, women who wished to free themselves from the care of children so that they could work outside the home had frequently turned to the orphanage. A secondary income that would permit them to do without a salary and still have their children at home would keep them captive to child care while simultaneously protecting them against life beyond the walls of the family home.

The debate soon turned from pensions for widows and needy mothers to the question of family allowances. The Jesuit Léon Lebel was the most enthusiastic advocate, publishing three pamphlets on the subject between 1927 and 1929.[90] He studied the various systems in force in Europe, dismissed objections that they represented socialism or state interference, and argued that such payments represented a solution to the problem of inadequate salaries, especially for large families. These allowances, paid progressively beginning with the third child, would be neither a salary nor charity but "repayment for outstanding service rendered to both society and to employers."[91] Lebel appeared before the Montpetit Commission in 1931 to argue for family allowances. He was to have the support of numerous nationalists and members of the clergy with natalist convictions throughout his entire campaign. Father Émile Clouthier, who viewed large families as an industrial asset, called for allowances to be paid by employers.[92] Writing in *L'Action française*, Hermas Bastien hoped that "compensation to the head of the household would repay him for the services he has rendered to society."[93] The father, as breadwinner, was worthy of such compensation.

A wage supplement would be more than a reward; it would act to encourage reproduction. The missionary and colonizer Georges M. Bilodeau, in discussing remedies for the economic crisis, expressed certain of his concerns, calling for family allowances in order to discourage the limitation of family size because "our most eminent men have come from our large families."[94] Despite his suspicion of the state, Henri Bourassa, the member from Labelle, accepted the principle of aid to large families. In the House of Commons he was, moreover, a warm supporter of every measure favouring the traditional family. In 1927 he congratulated the federal government for its announcement of tax relief for parents of children under twenty-one.[95]

The father, the worker, deserved recognition for the services he rendered to society, but the mother, not just as widow or breadwinner, soon became an object of solicitude. The medical profession, always closely concerned with the condition of child-bearing women, asked for maternal insurance to supply a payment to pregnant women that would permit them to have household help as well as maternity payments following delivery.[96] To preserve the family circle and to eliminate the quite common practice of widows having to board their children out in order to take care of them, the Union Nationale government passed an act in 1937 to aid needy mothers.[97] Universal family allowances would have to wait until the federal government's initiative following World War Two. When they did come into being, Maurice Duplessis was opposed to the payments being made to the mothers, but the concerted action of Quebec women convinced the federal government to issue the cheques in their names.[98] Probably because of the fertility of Quebec families, the polls of the period indicate that these benefits were very popular, especially among the population of child-bearing age. Whether it was inspired by certain politicians interested in encouraging a high rate of birth or whether it was intended as an acknowledgement of a valuable social service, a monthly sum payable to the mother recognized her age-old role in the care of children.

While certain laws and social measures might reinforce the traditional place of the mother in the home, it was still vital to maintain the family structure, which was seen to be under threat. As right-thinking people deplored the erosion of traditional values and institutions by modern life and industrial society, experts emerged to direct women and men in their family duties. Particular instruction pertained to each specific role. Dr. Joseph-Ambroise Beaudouin, director of the École d'hygiène sociale attached to the University of Montreal, wished to include child care in domestic science education since education had to prepare girls for "their principal mission . . . of raising a large family."[99] According to his colleague, Gaston Lapierre, the last year of school or convent was the best moment "to gain a hold over the future mother" and teach her notions of baby care "before prejudices can get to her."[100]

The development of a classical high school course for girls (parallel to that followed by boys) was greeted by considerable criticism. It was feared that higher education could only be at the expense of the genuine and proper education of young women – education in preparation for marriage and motherhood. At the Semaine sociale du Canada of 1927, Ferdinand Roy maintained that only 20 per cent of female students actually benefited from being educated to the higher standard, while the "true education" of the other 80 per cent was being sacrificed. In his view, the "excessive and general" education of girls led to the undermining of paternal and maternal authority.[101] Even those who were promoting a more advanced standard for girls tried to reassure the sceptics. Gaëtane de Montreuil, a journalist at *La Presse,* was bold enough to support co-education because girls who were at school with boys displayed "keener and more open minds." Realistic and up-to-date, she desired the education of women because a large number of them would have to work for a living and she hoped that they could pursue a career of their own choosing. Their vocation as women would not be endangered because "it is pointless to keep telling them to stay home and raise their children. It is their fondest dream."[102] Unfortunately, the writer did not elaborate on what she perceived to be the causes of this domestic fervour – nature, conditioning, or the monotony of the jobs open to women in 1925. As far as her colleague "Fadette" was concerned, advanced instruction was a risk and ought never rob young girls of those basic qualities "so necessary to raise them to the heights of their maternal task."[103] These qualities may perhaps have been innate, but they had to be monitored and cultivated right up to the moment of motherhood.

No matter what instincts the mother might be provided with, she still had to serve her apprenticeship. Public health experts especially laid great stress on pre- and post-natal courses for women. Post-natal follow-up by nurses was seen as essential if the newborn was to survive an infant mortality rate of more than one in ten. Demography, or the future of the race as it was then called, was also a political question. In a speech deploring emigration and encouraging the repatriation of Quebec émigrés from the United States, Athanase David pushed the necessity for teaching the mothers of tomorrow how to care for their children: "That will be the finest repatriation that we can achieve."[104] These mothers, though worthy of the most respectful worship, still had to be instructed in the art of preserving their children.

Advertisement for free information on modern child care. From *La Revue moderne* (juin 1932).

At the end of the 1930s the chaplain of the Jeunesse ouvrière catholique, Father Henri Roy, OMI, conceived the notion of instructing engaged couples before they embarked on a life of mutual harmony and permanence – a preparation for marriage course. Inspired by Pius IX's encyclical, *Casti Connubii,* and following an extensive consultation with doctors, lawyers, and members of the clergy, the Oblate Fathers of Mary Immaculate launched a pilot course destined for twenty-five couples who would take their vows in Notre Dame Church. The instruction was given over to specialists: a lawyer explained to the couples the intricacies of the Civil Code; a doctor revealed the mysteries of biology separately to each sex. The first complete course ended in a blaze of glory – a nuptial Mass on July 23, 1939, for 106 couples who had received a mark of at least 60 per cent on fifteen exams. Monsignor Georges Gauthier celebrated the sacrament in De Lorimier Stadium in Montreal before 25,000 parents and spectators who had come from as far away as Ontario and Nova Scotia for the event.[105] This great popular celebration presented these couples as an example. Their unions would be stable and fertile because they had been prepared. You could not simply get married; you had to learn the rules and benefit from the teaching of those wiser than yourself. In its reliance on experts, the Church was only following a tendency that had been established in civil life for several decades.

Various organizations, acting out of humanitarian and natalist considerations, appeared to teach and oversee the care of infants. Canon Pailleur founded the Association des Gouttes de lait (Milk Drop Association) in his working-class parish in 1910. Dr. Séverin Lachapelle quickly became its chairman and it began to receive government support in 1922.[106] In 1912, Mrs. Henry Hamilton started Assistance maternelle to "give aid to poor mothers before, during, and after the birth of their child."[107] The needy mothers were provided with house

Mass marriages, De Lorimier Stadium, Montreal, July 23, 1939. ANQ,
Conrad Poirier, P48/13/3707, P48/13/3711.

visits, free attention from a doctor and visiting nurses, a layette and provisions, and, above all, advice about how to take care of the baby. The intrusion of specialists and experts into their lives was, so to speak, the price the poor paid for services rendered: "In a way, the aid we provide the families gives us the right to advise them about hygiene and cleanliness, to urge them to be economical and, where necessary, to show them how to balance their budgets."[108] In 1924 the agency started a social service employing forty women to visit poor families. In the same year it opened a small hospital on Cherrier Street. One hundred thirty-nine births were registered there in 1926. The service dealt with 929 women in 1929 and, presumably as a result of the depression, 4,000 in 1933.[109] All of these organizations were set up not merely to serve the needs of the mother and her infant but, even more, to educate her in child care and proper standards of housekeeping. A well-run household was considered essential to sustaining a united family whose members would prefer to stay at home rather than wander off to the movies, the taverns, or other pernicious places, and the mother was responsible for maintaining an attractive home, however humble it might be.

Among the mechanisms developed to further the training of the mother-wife, we must mention the school programs and the institutions specific to girls, for their education was never to proceed to the detriment of their femininity and their future vocation. Well before the First World War, homemaking courses were part of the curriculum of almost every Western nation. Housekeeping skills were inculcated as early as possible; in both public and private schools, these materials were added to the basic program. A network of agricultural domestic science institutions had been developing beyond the primary-school level since 1882, and in 1906 a provincial domestic science school was established in Montreal under the sponsorship of the FNSJB.[110] Marie Lacoste Gérin-Lajoie paid particular attention to the training of future mothers. She would have liked to see the pediatric and child-care courses given by the Grey Nuns made part of the senior high school course in addition to a required practical stint in a nursery, in order to make up for "the lack of preparation of mothers for their maternal vocation."[111] There were indeed differences in the education of girls and boys, especially in the cities where each sex had its separate schools and even specialized schools where girls could complete their education with an eye to their future vocation as mother of the family.

There was no question of teaching young women trades that would place them in competition with men of their own age. The depression highlighted the expectations society had for women of the working class. The federal and provincial governments funded three training centres in Quebec for unemployed women to prepare them to re-enter

Housekeeping course for unemployed women at the YMCA, 1938. ANQ, Conrad Poirier, P48/8/2275.

the work force. Dressed in blue and white uniforms, they took courses in housekeeping, cooking, dressmaking, cleaning, laundry, care of furniture, waiting on table, cleanliness and "personal appearance," home care of the sick, and the care and feeding of children. While all of this might qualify them to become mistresses of their own establishments, the students were hardly guaranteed that a job awaited them. Unsurprisingly, 20 per cent of the women left the program compared to only 2 per cent of men who dropped out of their course at these training centres.[112] The first concern of educators, in such training schemes as well as in the schools, remained the ultimate vocation of women as wives and mothers.

Mothers, trained for motherhood and under the watchful eye of the social services, must not be allowed to turn away from their domestic duties to engage in activities outside the family. Politics was therefore closed to them on the pretext that such interests would cause them to neglect their homes. In a letter published in *Le Devoir* in February, 1922, Monsignor Roy congratulated the Anti-Women's Suffrage Committee for protecting "traditional responsibilities" under threat by the involvement of women in political action.[113]

Henri Bourassa is probably the best-known anti-feminist lay spokesman of the period. In his opinion, those feminine qualities, like intuition, which were so precious an asset in the home, made the female "less capable than a man to determine the government." Her moral superiority, "when sustained by motherhood," far from giving her an edge in political judgement, could never raise her to the level of the male in public affairs.[114] The discourse on motherhood was used to justify depriving women of the right to vote. In 1918, as the House of Commons was debating the women's suffrage bill, the members from Quebec were opposed because they viewed it as a "danger to the birth rate."[115] Charles Fournier, the member from Bellechasse, made it quite clear: "If the birth rate in Canada is to be maintained, our women must be retained in their proper sphere."[116] Those virtues that destined women for maternity and all the duties associated with it were precisely what disqualified them from participation in the public sphere.

A number of different groups had been calling for the franchise for women since the end of the nineteenth century; the FNSJB, founded in 1907, campaigned for women's suffrage until Cardinal Bégin issued a ban in 1922. In 1928, the League for Women's Rights, founded by Thérèse Casgrain, took over. Idola Saint-Jean had already begun the Alliance canadienne pour le vote des femmes du Québec the previous year. These two large organizations collaborated on a number of occasions to confront the majority of those elected as Liberals or Conservatives (and Union Nationale after 1936).

The immensely high value attached to family life made it possible to accept being confined within it. A professional writer like "Fadette" seemed wholly convinced that no woman would wish to escape the subjugation that accompanied motherhood. At the Semaine sociale du Canada in 1923 she exclaimed, "When kings and people combine to enfranchise woman, she will return to her benign slavery on the day she becomes a mother, and the beautiful miracle, constantly renewed, is that she loves her slavery, lovingly kisses the chains that bind her, like a holy object. God has willed it so; our freedom will mean the end of the world!"[117]

Both supporters and opponents of the vote for women based their arguments on inherent maternal qualities. The debates in the Legislative Assembly that accompanied the twelve bills in favour of women's suffrage between 1927 and 1940 illustrate very clearly the way in which members might use conventional wisdom about the nature of women.[118] Joseph-Édouard Fortin, the member from Beauce, in 1934 summed up the fears of his colleagues, who were more concerned with demography than political equality: "Votes for women is a foremost reprehensible part of feminism; it is the first symptom of that contagious disease which can destroy the wonderful birth rate of our homes."[119] The following year Dr. Pierre Gauthier invoked his scientific knowledge in affirming that "it is by virtue of the natural principle of the infant's need for his mother that we would prevent women from being given the right to vote."[120]

The most effective course for the suffragists was to refute their adversaries by basing their arguments on the same premises to show that women's special qualities made them particularly qualified to select their political representatives. Idola Saint-Jean and Thérèse Casgrain used this strategy to convince the authorities and public opinion that persons who were devoted to family values, children's education, and moral purity could make only a positive contribution to political debate.

Not only excluded from the Legislative Assembly, women were also prevented from studying medicine and law as well as from engaging in a whole host of other occupations. As Premier Alexandre Taschereau put it, there was no need to have lady doctors and lady lawyers in order to achieve Quebec's national destiny, and "the true mission of women is to remain faithful to our ancestral traditions, to their role as Queen of the Home, to their charitable and philanthropic works, and to their labours of love and self-sacrifice." He implored them, "Please, remain our superiors. As such you are, due to your heart and your devotion."[121] If they were married, all paid work outside the home was viewed with suspicion. They were sometimes involved in organizations of women workers, timidly in the employees' associations organized by the FNSJB, more confidently in the unions. But there they remained submissive to the decisions taken by their male colleagues, strike leaders who ruled on the validity of their demands and determined under what conditions they would return to work.[122] During labour disputes, women were on the picket line and the more radical of them were swiftly brought to book by the authorities. Single women were most active in union activities; if the mother of a family were to demonstrate publicly, the authorities were quick to recall her to her duty. During the loggers' strike in Noranda in 1933, the judge directed Mrs. George Evanik, who had been arrested for illegal assembly following the reading of the Riot Act, to stay home and take care of her children.[123] It was not just that maternal duty had to have priority over public involvement; it was, in fact, an impediment to any such commitment. On behalf of the exalted role of mother, women were excluded from politics and the learned professions, and even from positions of responsibility in the very organizations that represented their interests.

This whole discussion of the essential nature of women did not remain innocently in the realm of theory. It found expression in controls and prohibitions designed to limit the scope of women's activities and to confine them to a situation of oppression. The dominant normative discourse and its apparatus to encourage conformity and repress dissent fit into an economic and social context that was evolving over two decades. Nevertheless, it does not appear that economic fluctuations, unemployment figures, or population movements found expression in any noticeable modifications in the image of woman and the definition of appropriate behaviour. In 1936, eighteen years after the portrait of women drawn by Monsignor Paquet in his articles on feminism, publisher Albert Lévesque devoted an entire number of *L'Almanach de la langue française* to the French-Canadian woman. After deploring the lack of intellectual awareness and the indifference of women to public life, it was agreed that "she sought her consolation in contemplating her crown of children." [124] It would require a study of much greater length to identify what gradual changes may have been taking place in the image of the ideal woman. Over two decades, every pronouncement on the maternal role, that primordial role that defined the sphere in which the Quebec mother passed her life, was marked with a sameness bordering on monotony.

3

Sexuality

The Normative Discourse

The wild years after the First World War are associated with a time of upheaval in morals and social behaviour that caused many people to view the period as *les années folles,* the crazy years. The return to "normality" following demobilization, the closing of the war plants, and the influenza epidemic were blamed for opening the floodgates that had heretofore dammed up sexuality in Quebec. Before examining the apocalyptic discourse of the period, it is a good idea to remind ourselves of the sexual ideal professed by the clergy, the medical profession, and others who defined social behaviour.

In this ideal sexuality, virginity remained the "sublime way"[1] preferred, at least since the Council of Trent (1545-1563), above all other possibilities and extolled in convents, at religious retreats for young women, and everywhere in pious literature. Virginity ideally was to be preserved within the walls of the convent, but "in the world" would do for those who lacked a vocation. Despite the exaltation of motherhood and the popular denigration of the old maid, the Church did not grant marriage the highest marks. The fact remains, nevertheless, that most did not achieve the sublime: in 1921, 12.1 per cent of women aged forty-five or over were unmarried and 2.2 per cent of adult women were in religious orders, that is, 9.1 per cent of all unmarried women, while the others had espoused "the common way" of marriage.[2]

The majority of Quebec women, preferring to embrace the life of the flesh, turned to the institution and sacrament of marriage. Regardless of the force of the pro-maternal discourse, it was a choice not without its pitfalls. Teenagers were provided with the words of Saint Alphonsus Liguori: "Married people may be holy in spirit but not in body."[3] Reproduction was one of the two intentions of the conjugal act; the other, the relief of pressing sexual urges not to be satisfied outside the bonds of holy matrimony, meant that sexuality, in essence, heterosexuality, was to be confined to marriage.

Every pre-marital sexual transgression was condemned by the Church, often with the endorsement of the medical profession. The question of purity was so important that Father Victorin Germain composed a catechism specifically devoted to the Sixth and Ninth Commandments as a complement to the official catechism, in which he details all the dangers to which the human body exposes the faithful. He did, nevertheless, concede that "all parts of the human body are not dangerous to see or to touch; one must, from the point of view of an occasion of sin, discriminate among decent, less decent, and indecent parts." He thus intended to put his readers on their guard against lust, sexual pleasure, and immodesty.[4]

Male masturbation, associated with sexual perversion, had long been condemned. But confessors also recognized that the practice was not confined to men alone. Physicians, while admitting that these "unnatural acts" were rare among women, viewed female masturbation as evidence of a depravity and degradation less excusable than for men because women did not have even "the semblance of the excuse afforded by an ardent sexual nature, one that is violent and brutal, which for some men passes for necessity."[5] It was, moreover, assumed that women, endowed by nature with less energy than men, found it easier to remain chaste.

Modesty was a virtue that would serve to protect this chastity, shielding young women from the desire to exercise their sexuality before marriage. The weakest, of course, would always fall, but the lapse would pass unnoticed as long as the sinner was not caught in the act or did not end up pregnant. Discretion was absolutely essential to avoid scandal and protect one's reputation. The measures taken to hide a premarital pregnancy – leaving home, entering an institution, changing one's name – merely indicate the consequences to the pregnant woman and her family that would follow from a tarnished reputation. The kind of childbirth termed "illegitimate" attested to behaviour primarily associated with the poorer classes and that would condemn unwed mothers to a life of failure. In an article on the "classification of the poverty-stricken," the social worker Albert Chevalier placed unmarried mothers in the category of "social discards," among the "involuntary poor."[6] In 1930 the social affairs expert Arthur Saint-Pierre, examining the bond between mother and child, commented realistically on "the kind of repugnance which unwed motherhood still inspires" and mentioned the "double burden of a damaged reputation and a child."[7] It is hardly surprising that the vast majority of unmarried mothers left their children in a crèche.

For young women from middle-class families, giving up their children was not an economic necessity but served to protect the family honour. That was the reason provided by those novelists who broached the subject. *La Chair décevante (The Deceiving Flesh)*, published in 1931 by Jovette Bernier, and *Soeur ou fiancée (Sister or Bride-to-be)* in 1932, by Dr. René de Cotret, both tell the story of an unmarried mother and her son.[8] Both books suggest the immense importance of hiding "irregular" births. In the novel by René de Cotret, the doctor asks the parents to send their daughter to a "hospital for nervous complaints." Although the young woman hopes to keep her baby, the doctor discourages her by calling on the "honour of the family," which she has endangered by "the disgrace of this birth."[9] Jovette Bernier's heroine, after leaving her son to be raised in the country, retrieves him when he is five years old, passing him off as the son of the man she has since married.[10] In real life as in fiction, it required the complicity of the doctor, the priest, and the immediate family to guarantee that conduct so fraught with distressing consequences might remain secret.

Even without the evidence of a childbirth, the loss of virginity would lead to a loss of social standing. In popular parlance, those who, whether through their own fault or not, lacked the requisite hymen were termed "debauched." Reputation was universally emphasized: young women who had lost theirs would never make a proper match and were in danger of being condemned to spinsterhood.

Extramarital affairs were similarly severely prohibited. In this case, the obligation to observe the Ninth Commandment bound both sexes equally, even if, in practice, there were some who judged the fault of the woman to be much the more serious. This question became relevant during the divorce debate in 1925. Senators Chapais and Béïque both viewed female adultery with the greatest seriousness because it could taint the paternal inheritance.[11] When women's suffrage came up for discussion one more time in the Legislative Assembly, Deputy Arthur Bélanger, M.D., trotted out the old adage once again: "The identity of the father is a matter of belief; that of the mother is a certainty."[12] The adulterous woman compromised the familial heritage and paraded a liberty that was doubly denied her as woman and as wife.

The code was simple: no sexual activity outside the bounds of marriage. The post-war convulsions might, it seemed, render the application of this code difficult, and there was a wide-scale denunciation of everything that might aid the descent into debauchery. In 1919, Monsignor Bruchési published a pastoral letter "On the Evils of the Present Moment"[13] and launched an appeal to the elite classes, to journalists, and to members of women's organizations to join the Ligue des Bonnes Moeurs (the Morality League). The relaxation of morals that was the

Dubious products promised ways to achieve the ideal feminine form. *La Revue moderne* (février 1925).

focus of attack manifested itself especially in fashion and in leisure activities, inspired by foreign influences like Americanism and naturalism. The influence of the United States and its disastrous consequences were the subject of an entire number of the *Revue dominicaine* in 1937. In it, one of the authors denounced the "insolent liberty of American manners."[14] This fear of Americanization, while it remained primarily a concern of the elite, was not wholly without foundation if one takes into account the cultural exchanges and population movements between Quebec and the United States.

Fashion, a pre-eminent American export, achieved an importance probably never before equalled for so large a number of women. Women's magazines and the movies circulated the latest word on height of hemline or depth of decolletage. Thanks to mass-produced clothing and the Eaton's catalogue, everyone seemed to be wearing the

Beer advertised as an aid to healthy fetus development. *La Revue moderne* (novembre 1931).

newest fashions, fashions that were all too frequently deemed immodest by the Pope and the bishops, and then by the various parish organizations that refereed questions of modesty.

In 1927, the bishops published a pastoral letter "On Naturalism and the Weakening of Morality." The FNSJB created an indecent fashion committee and Madame F.-X. Dupuis protested against women's fashions in the pages of *La Bonne Parole*. The article is interesting in that it stresses the class difference that accompanies its strictures. Rich women would have less to fear from embracing fashion while the middle class was prey to its ravages because "in order to adorn themselves, mothers have been known to sink to the most sordid and vile occupations and to dishonour their families and subject them to privation upon privation."[15] Thus, bondage to fashion might not lead directly to immorality through the display of too much naked flesh, but indirectly it would, due to the means to which certain less fortunate women might stoop to satisfy their sense of style.

The clergy continued to condemn the immodesty of feminine clothing. In 1938, the Canadian Eucharistic Congress afforded the bishops the opportunity to remind their flocks of the principles of good conduct in dress. Those who were called "persons of sex" would not be permitted to approach the altar if dressed in too casual or too worldly a manner: "they should thus wear a garment sufficiently high at the neck and which covers the arms to the wrist and which reaches at least below the knee. Best of all will be those women who add at least an ample overcoat," even if the Congress were to take place in the summer.[16] We can only be struck by the contrast between this proposed costume and the image projected by the flapper, that liberated young woman of the twenties.

The subject was of such importance to all elements of society that even Julien Saint-Michel, who wrote about such social questions as child labour, women's suffrage, and the exploitation of workers, also devoted several articles to fashion. She lauded the emancipation of the female body in less constraining garments, which were "symbols of a greater emancipation." She nevertheless deplored those martyrs to fashion who had to follow it at any cost and castigated what she saw as excesses: overdone make-up, fox-fur collars worn year round, and any style that exposed bodily imperfections, unsightly forms, or bow legs.[17] The intention of Saint-Michel's comments is, of course, at variance with those other social critics who were primarily preoccupied with controlling sexuality and safeguarding modesty in dress.

If fashion was capable of stirring vile thoughts, vile desires, and vile acts, what about other pastimes that, much more frequently than before the war, took place outside the home? Dances in which entwined couples risked touching each other too closely or made provocative gestures were labelled lascivious. Dancing was prohibited altogether in certain dioceses; in Montreal, warnings were issued against certain dances. These prohibitions, far from losing their force over time, were repeated by the bishops and reiterated from the pulpit throughout the entire period.[18]

How to isolate Quebec from jazz, the Charleston, and most of all, from the infamous tango when the idols of the screen were attracting an

An approved, appropriately modest, bathing costume. *La Bonne Parole* (juin 1939).

entire generation of young people who wanted more and more to spend an afternoon, or if possible, an evening far from the watchful parental eye? Although Hollywood films of the twenties were still silent, they could nevertheless, according to the bishops, "awaken the most per-verse and gross instincts of a fallen nature."[19] Equally reviled were all those places where pleasure-mad youth could meet one another unchaperoned. Among these were the beaches and public pools, which inspired the bishops to try to limit them to persons of the same sex and to warn against the teaching of swimming "to persons of the female sex by masculine instructors."[20] *La Bonne Parole* drew attention to a mod-est bathing suit available to all at Dupuis Frères department store.[21] Even winter sports such as skating, skiing, and snowshoeing "involve particular occasions of moral peril, especially when both sexes partici-pate."[22] Finally, what could be said about "automobilism," which encouraged young men and women to undertake extended excursions without supervision?[23] Occasions of sin (of the flesh, naturally) multi-plied with the number of leisure activities that evaded the vigilant eye of parents and chaperones; for young women, the consequences of a lapse would prove irremediable.

New currents of thought underlay this invasion of immoral fashions and distractions. Naturalism was especially denounced, attacked by Pius XI in 1929 in his encyclical on Christian education. "This passion for enjoyment which glorifies the flesh" arises from a materialism that elevates nature at the expense of spirit and would be responsible for a relaxation of morals.[24] Another reviled "ism" was "*garçonnisme*," which encouraged girls to behave and even dress like boys. This con-cept had its source in the famous novel *La Garçonne* (1921) by the French author Victor Margueritte, which advocated sexual liberation for both sexes.[25] The clergy flailed away at the emancipation of women and its dire consequences. According to Father Panneton, author of a little pamphlet on the subject, "the *garçonne* drags mankind to the bot-tom of the pit dug by Eve's sin."[26] *Garçonnisme* was the fruit of an emancipation based on the equality of the sexes, which would lead to a confusion of roles, the ultimate expression of which would be the wearing of male garments. Femininity in all its external manifestations was a defence against immodesty and loose behaviour, in short, against the exercise of sexuality outside of marriage.

Why did it seem impossible to trust these young women, raised from infancy in the principles of the Catholic religion? Had they not been warned sufficiently to resist new temptations? Sex education was largely non-existent, ignorance being presumed to guarantee inno-cence. In her autobiography Claire Martin, who was born in 1914, lifts the veil from the prudery of an education dominated by the sin of impu-rity: "Our sin! In Quebec, we only had but one sin."[27] If she was not always altogether devoid of knowledge, the young woman was often represented as weak or provocative, or as easy prey.

Certain handbooks were as much interested in giving information about the elementary facts of sexuality as they were in warning their female readers against the perils that menaced them. Father Germain is explicit about the causes of "illegitimate" births: "Any close friendship between persons of different sexes which takes place without a third party present . . . may lead to a like degradation."[28] But even the greatest vigilance may be thwarted. In a story inspired by his chaplaincy at the foundling hospital in Quebec, he cites a mother who asked him, "How is it that after my husband and I have done all we could to watch closely over our child, she winds up in the same place as girls without supervision or education?" that is, in the Miséricorde hospital for single mothers. To which the chaplain responded: "I have noticed that irreparable disgrace is the punishment for either the illicit loves of the parents before marriage or else for the reprehensible limitation of conceptions. . . ." To which the mother replied: "In our case, it was preventing a family."[29] Thus might the consequences of a sin be passed along to successive generations. In another tale, a father is likewise punished by his daughter's sin because he was the owner of a hotel denounced by the parish priest as a house of prostitution.

Father Germain is not the only one to place the burden of responsibility for their daughters' behaviour on the parents. Judge Geoffrion attributed the seduction of daughters and their recruitment into prostitution to parental negligence.[30] *La Bonne Parole* issued a warning to parents of daughters who might be tempted to reply to job offers that could turn out to be merely a screen for the white slave trade.[31] In *Le Monde ouvrier,* Julien Saint-Michel spoke out against the ignorance in which these little babes in the wood were kept. Closer to young working women, she was aware of the sexual harassment to which they were exposed and of the seduction that lay in wait for them. Sex education adapted to post-war circumstances, she believed, could only provide some protection against dangers, accidents, and disgrace.[32]

Married women also had to be protected against knowledge considered inappropriate if not actually unwholesome. Thus the indiscretions of the husband were concealed even when they affected the health of the wife. In a series of lectures on dermato-venereology, Dr. L.-M. Pautrier advised physicians how to treat women infected by their husbands. A patient whose husband has a venereal disease should be examined under the pretext of a uterine inflammation. If she is infected and her husband does not want to own up, the doctor should treat her for "anemia." The mother also should not be told that her minor daughter has contracted the disease extra-genitally. In the name of maintaining professional secrecy, only the father, presumably the agent of infection, would be informed of the contamination of other members of the family.[33] Even in regard to her own personal hygiene, the female had to be protected from the sexual realities that surrounded her.

Despite all the means employed to safeguard women's innocence and ignorance, certain realities imposed themselves, either from reading the newspapers or when stepping beyond determined geographical limits. It was common knowledge that there existed a category of women who, defying every prohibition, managed to exercise their sexuality without being married and with no intention of becoming pregnant. No one was unaware that prostitution was an element of life in large urban centres. It is useful to pause for a moment to consider the discourse concerning the prostitute, the woman who was seen to embody the most profound degeneration and whose very name was used more often as a metaphor than as an actual fact. Dr. Antoine-Hector Desloges, an eminent specialist in venereal disease, proclaimed that "from the moment a woman enters into an extra-marital relationship, that woman is a prostitute," a "will-o'-the-wisp" who cannot be trusted because she will go from lover to lover.[34] Nevertheless, even if the term "whore" might have been attached to any unmarried woman who had lost her virginity, prostitution itself refers to a precise condition of existence.

Several thousand women, located primarily in Montreal, participated in the sex trade in Quebec. The notorious red-light district stretched between Sherbrooke and Craig streets, from Bleury on the west to St. Denis on the east, but was particularly concentrated south of St. Catherine and east of St. Lawrence Boulevard. The prostitute in this period was viewed more as a victim than as someone who was wilfully perverse. The repeated cliché, which for some corresponded to a life experience, saw prostitution as the inevitable result of a slide that began with an initial mistake.[35] After a stay at the Hôpital de la Miséricorde, rejected by her friends and family, failing to find employment because of her past, the young single mother would become the victim of the procurer and the pimp prowling for "new stock." In fact, a number of brothel inmates skipped the step of motherhood – unable to find domestic work when they got to the city and attracted by the prospect of earnings far higher than the female minimum wage, they found themselves in a profession that always had room for more.

Sexual traffic was ascribed to male nature far more often than to female corruption. This apparently aberrant female behaviour, however, demanded some explanation. In an age with a weakness for scientific interpretation, a predisposition for sexual deviance was found in heredity. In 1919, Carrie Derick, professor of biology at McGill University and chair of a committee of the Montreal Local Council of Women (MLCW) on mental deficiency, fell under the sway of eugenics theory and insisted on the connection between mental deficiency and depravity. According to Derick, 60 to 70 per cent of Canadian prostitutes were feeble-minded.[36] This assertion was repeated by physicians and social reformers absorbed with the problem. Grace Ritchie-England, the first female doctor in Quebec and member of the executive of the MLCW; Antoine-Hector Desloges, director of the anti-venereal disease campaign in Quebec and director-general of the psychiatric hospitals and reform and industrial schools; Alfred K. Haywood of the Montreal General Hospital; the hygienist J.-A. Beaudouin: all mentioned the feeble-mindedness of prostitutes.[37] How accurate these judgements were is difficult to ascertain. Perhaps these observers experienced a certain difficulty in imagining a woman of ordinary intelligence engaging in work they found repugnant, or perhaps working in such a trade would result in a mental collapse? For Carrie Derick, feeble-mindedness was the cause, not the result, of the delinquency.[38]

In any population there always exists a certain percentage of individuals who are more or less deficient intellectually. In the case of young women who are affected in this way, it is quite possible that they might more readily become victims of abuse or, with a poorer chance of finding a job, might end up in a trade where their intelligence was less important than their anatomy. Whether or not they were intellectually handicapped, many of them were certainly illiterate according to the testimony of Nathan Gordon, crown prosecutor of the Recorder's Court, and of Roch Sauvé, the chief of police, both of whom were in daily contact with the more disreputable members of society.[39] For the social reformers, the intellectual deficiencies of prostitutes made them into double victims in need of protection.

Not all prostitutes were lacking in intellect or were victims of early seduction. Those priests and doctors who were in contact with them had to admit there were social and economic causes for their occupation. In 1925, the Coderre Police Commission provided the opportunity for certain witnesses to explain the motives impelling so many women to trade in their sexual services. Father Henri Gauthier of Saint Jacques parish remarked that when, on his parochial visits, he asked prostitutes to "cease their unspeakable trade," he got the answer, "No way – this is how we earn our living."[40] Chief of police Joseph Tremblay made the same point when he discussed the condition of female workers who worked in shops for six or seven dollars a week, and Dr. Desloges particularly blamed the unhealthy lodgings from which the young women sought to escape in whatever way they might.[41] For Julien Saint-Michel, the journalist from *Le Monde ouvrier,* prostitution was directly linked to poverty and to the low salaries that did not allow young women to acquire the goods that society encouraged them to consume.[42] Although prostitution was in direct contradiction to all the relevant sexual standards of behaviour, a number of men nevertheless considered it a necessary evil. A whole category of women might be "sacrificed" to protect the ideal and they would be more or less excused on the grounds of their feeble intellects, their economic situation, and the demands of masculine sexuality.

If everyone who delivered an opinion on the subject tended to view prostitutes primarily as victims, it is still possible to distinguish various degrees of willingness in their choice of occupation. A certain number, which was probably inflated, found themselves caught in the meshes of the white slave trade. Drawn in against their will, they were trapped in a system difficult to escape. Then there were those who, ostracized following a public disgrace, were already seen as sliding down the slope that led to the street or the brothel. Lastly, a final group, faced with the prospect of being extremely badly paid as domestics or unskilled labour, chose a more dangerous profession, but one that offered immediate economic advantage. According to the special interest of each commentator, the solution lay in the abolition of the white slave trade and sanctions against pimps and madams, or the prevention of "illegitimate" pregnancies, or the relief of the economic situation of women.

Regardless of what was responsible for their condition or their trade according to the perspective from which they were viewed, prostitutes were marginalized, strictly confined within their own circumscribed space. Their clients, and the reformers, could penetrate into their world, but the reverse was unthinkable. An anecdote in the biography of Dr. Norman Bethune illustrates the degree of scandal the presence of a prostitute might cause in the "wrong" place. Bethune arrived at a dinner party accompanied by a prostitute, to whom he gave some food and a drink. After she had eaten her meal, he announced to the astonished guests, "Now, ladies and gentlemen, I shall return her to where she came from, to the streets and to degradation."[43] Whether Bethune wanted to heighten his host's social awareness, or whether he merely wished to raise some bourgeois hackles, his gesture shocked not because of how he was using the woman but because he was violating social etiquette. The two worlds might comfortably co-exist, but her world must never be publicly recognized, especially when ladies were present.

The prostitute did not merely represent the victim of male lust or of economic disadvantage, but embodied as well the pathology linked to those diseases she might contract and transmit. One could not deal with prostitution without raising the question of contagion. "Prostitution is the source and centre of all venereal disease," Dr. J.M.E. Prévost asserted in his *Ce que chacun devrait savoir* (*What every man ought to know*).[44] This notion was repeated by the doctors working for the Quebec Provincial Health Service as well as by those who undertook the examination of prostitutes for the police or at the Montreal General Hospital.[45] Because those who were infected were sick they had to be treated, and the government, having become aware of the extent of venereal infection through the examination of recruits during the war, allocated significant sums to the anti-venereal disease campaign. Nevertheless, certain doctors maintained punitive attitudes and would, in the name of public morality, restrict the treatment of the infected. Dr. L.-A. Gagnier published *Droits et devoirs de la médecine et des médecins canadiens-français* (*The Rights and Duties of Medicine and French-Canadian Physicians*) in 1926, in which he expressed his reservations about the clinics where decent women infected by their husbands might rub elbows with their shameful sisters. He especially desired that fees be imposed because "it would be rendering a poor service to the sick to ease their access [to the clinic]. It is far better that they do a little something to atone for their sins."[46] The attitude of Dr. Gagnier is not unique, but it directly contradicts the efforts of the public health professionals who were doing their best to track down illness and publicize information about treatment. In terms of the latter, if they could not cure, at least they might limit infection.

As deviant, victim, and agent of contamination, the prostitute provoked a discussion that renders transparent the double standard of morality. Of course, there was no unanimity about this double standard – officially, the Church held both men and women to the same ideals and the same prohibitions. Social pronouncements, however, departed from these monovalent rules and were more slyly tolerant of masculine deviations from them. Women who offended were rapidly reproved. Feminists, who advocated a uniform code of morality, called for equal penalties for those breaking the laws against prostitution, regardless of gender. When, in 1918, one of these women approached Judge Geoffrion to this effect, he ridiculed her for wanting to treat as criminals "those men who went [to a brothel] in a moment of weakness, these husbands and fathers." Six years later, he admitted that "I understood instantly that it was futile to discuss further any questions concerning amendments to the Civil Code with ladies."[47] Thus, yet again, these discussions are grounded in the legal and social practices that reflect the perceptions, the beliefs, and the prejudices surrounding female sexuality.

Normative Practices

Only in marriage might a woman express her sexuality – the husband was to enjoy exclusive rights to her, an exclusiveness guaranteed by pre-marital chastity, by a prolonged state of innocence, and by protection from the pitfalls characterizing modern life. Sexuality was hedged round with a thicket of prohibitions and markers clearly delimiting its expression, and legislation was enacted to protect potential victims and to punish assaults on sexual purity within the framework of both masculine and feminine requirements. Those organizations devoted to censorship, to a specifically female education, and to prevention and rehabilitation reinforced the legislative apparatus in order to maintain the social order in sexual relations.

The double standard that dictated the treatment dealt to victims of sexual crimes, to prostitutes and their clients, and to those suffering from venereal disease had long been enshrined in the Civil Code in force in Quebec. Therefore, the two sexes experienced very different consequences in the matter of adultery. Although the husband could cite simple adultery as grounds for separation, the wife would have to prove that the offence had taken place in the marital establishment in order to be granted a legal separation. When the Dorion Commission was formed in 1929 to inquire into the question of the civil rights of married women, the feminist members of the Alliance pour le vote des femmes du Québec asked that the grounds for obtaining a legal separation be made the same for both sexes. In its report, however, the Commission retained both the double standard and the quasi-impunity of the male adulterer.[48]

In its protective mode, legislation discouraged and punished sexual assaults. The Criminal Code prohibited all sexual relations with girls under fourteen years of age. Article 211 of the Code specifically forbade the seduction of young women between the ages of sixteen and eighteen by men older than eighteen: if the victim were of previously chaste character, the offender was liable to two years in prison. When the age of consent was raised in 1919 from sixteen to eighteen, despite the opposition of certain senators, the obligation of chastity was not specified for girls between fourteen and sixteen.[49] For those over sixteen, certain extenuating circumstances might, to an extent, excuse the loss of virginity – it was hardly unheard of for an engaged woman to yield to the importunities of her fiancé. To discourage the glib, breach of promise was a criminal offence if the fiancée was under twenty-one.

The law extended its protection to young women workers who were vulnerable to their bosses' advances. Whether because of their ignorance, the lack of parental supervision, or their dependency on their employers, young domestic workers were particularly at risk. An 1892 law made it a criminal offence for an employer to seduce or have illicit sexual relations with a woman in his employ younger than twenty-one who had been previously chaste. It was broadened in 1920 to include domestic employers along with the owners of factories and workshops.[50]

The legal machinery to preserve female virtue was in place, but if the judicial archives do provide some evidence of various transgressions they do not reveal much about the extent to which they might have occurred. The parents of a pregnant daughter would occasionally pursue the seducer who had promised to marry her, if only in the hope of recovering the cost of the pregnancy. A study of the seduction, rape, and indecent assault cases in Montreal during the 1930s indicates that often fewer than half of those accused were found guilty.[51] Sometimes there was insufficient evidence, sometimes the plaintiff failed to appear, but there was always humiliation for the victim, who had to provide proof of her previous chastity before sceptical lawyers and judges. The victim would be required to have behaved in an absolutely irreproachable way, and often the absence of parental surveillance was seen as the cause of her plight. A mother of nine, faced with working outside the home, was scolded for leaving her children in the house by themselves. The judge would reprimand the victims for their lack of caution: "Evidence has not been introduced as to whether or not she was informed in advance that he would be home alone."[52] A lawyer for the defence asked: "Had he already taken hold of your breasts? . . . Were those little kisses or big kisses?"[53] Under such circumstances, it would appear that only the most naive or most desperate of parents would appeal to the law, and one wonders if they were aware of what they were exposing their daughter to when they did so.

Prosecutions for rape were even less likely to succeed than cases of seduction that led to a pregnancy. The poor rate of conviction and light sentencing hardly served to discourage rape. The plaintiff found herself implicated in a crime – each case entailed the condemnation, humiliation, and punishment of the victim, whose reputation was tarnished and who often had to assume the consequences of enforced pregnancy. Both the laws and their application were founded on the double standard of morality in a world that demanded a vigilant control of female virtue. A fallen woman might have been unwilling and still earn the designation of "debauched." Victims of seduction or of rape experienced equal social disgrace.

Prostitution, which made an economic activity out of sexuality and involved the connivance of both sexes, was regulated by legislation that sought more to control than to deter. The concern in the first instance was to protect and defend innocent victims who might be drawn against their will into the net of sexual traffic. The international movement against the white slave trade at the end of the last century had its echoes in Canada. The legislators took a harsh tack, and procurers who incited to debauchery were liable to fourteen years in prison.[54] For those involved in the sex trade, the Criminal Code of Canada and the Quebec statutes established the limits of legal activities inside the brothels. It was criminal to be found inside a bawdy house (art. 228), to keep such a house (art. 229, sec. 1), or to be the knowing proprietor of premises used for this purpose (art. 229, sec. 1), which stipulation doomed to failure any action against the owners. In order to be able to issue injunctions against the owners, the government of Quebec passed an Act Concerning the Proprietors of Premises Used as Bawdy Houses in 1920, but it was a law almost impossible to enforce since ownership easily changed hands or was registered to a public company.[55]

If prostitutes were not directly affected by the legislation dealing with proprietors, they often risked being "found" in bawdy houses and arrested under article 229 or as debauched persons who "habitually frequent bawdy houses" under the Law Concerning the Police and Good Order.[56] Municipal regulations against vagrancy and loitering lay in wait for women who did not operate in brothels and whose activities became too evident.

There is a considerable space between what the law says and how it is applied. Rather than cracking down on every infraction of the law, the authorities did their best for decades to confine prostitution to an area where it might be more readily controlled. Montreal more or less tolerated the existence of brothels in its red-light district even if the question of their regulation and abolition might arise from time to time as it did in other major cities in Europe and North America. The 1925 police commission chaired by Judge Louis Coderre tried to deal with the supervised toleration of bawdy houses. The opposing parties to the debate, from abolitionists to regulators, appeared before the commissioners to express their points of view. It might be useful here to pause for a moment to understand the flow of ideas informing the legislators in this controversy.

Members of the clergy, social reformers, and feminists formed the core of those who wanted prostitution suppressed as far as practicable. Hardly any of them, however, called for the absolute closure of all the brothels, and most were of the opinion, like Father Gauthier, that prostitution could never be made to disappear completely from a large city like Montreal.[57] A group of mostly Anglophone reformers, the Committee of Sixteen, was especially concerned with commercialized vice, that is, transactions involving a third party who reaped the profits. The feminists, who were not called as witnesses before the Coderre Commission, were absolutely opposed to prostitution and insisted that the municipal authorities apply the rigour of the law and close down the houses. Marie Lacoste Gérin-Lajoie of the FNSJB, and Grace Ritchie-England of the MLCW met with the mayor of Montreal, Charles Duquette, to offer their help in putting an end to this era of toleration.[58] In this, they had the support of Judge Coderre, who in his report asked the police and the courts to leave no stone unturned in observing the law and eliminating prostitution from the city.

Diametrically opposite this group were the regulators, who favoured the segregation of prostitution into a single neighbourhood, the issuance of identification cards, and the medical examination of prostitutes. Recorder Amédée Geoffrion, Médéric Martin, the mayor of Montreal from 1914 to 1928, the union leader Gustave Francq, and Julien Saint-Michel, the journalist from *Le Monde ouvrier,* defended regulation of the brothels from an extreme position. Their arguments were based on the necessity to protect the public from the threat of venereal disease, the need to control the underworld connected with the brothels, and the demands of male nature, which, if it was thwarted, could lead to dire consequences for respectable young women.[59] Regulation had already been shown to be a failure in Paris, where it had not succeeded in curbing street prostitution, while it clashed head-on with Catholic and Protestant morality.

Between these two opposing camps lay an attitude of resigned toleration. While it was not talked about in great detail and was often accompanied by vague gestures of repression, toleration governed the trade in Montreal. The medical profession, the daily press, and the police were in favour of this hybrid system of control that allowed the brothel-keepers, their inmates, and their clients a degree of freedom in exchange for payoffs to the police and occasional arrests to mollify public opinion.

The law was also intended to protect society against infection on the part of prostitutes carrying venereal disease. Alerted during the war to the spread of these diseases, public health officers from every province met in Ottawa in 1919 to advise the government, which was about to establish a Department of Health. A huge anti-venereal disease campaign was launched the following year, with $200,000 of federal funds for the country as a whole added to an equal sum furnished by the provinces to establish laboratories and clinics as well as for lectures and advertising. The Quebec government created a provincial commission to combat venereal disease and, thanks to the support of the clergy and various social institutions, several thousand persons were found and treated. After the initial enthusiasm began to fade, federal grants started to taper off in 1924 and amounted to only $50,000 by 1938. A shift in governmental priorities rather than the abolition of the disease was accountable for the reduction in annual funding.[60]

Those infected were always free to seek treatment, but article 316a of the Criminal Code made it an offence knowingly to communicate a venereal disease. In addition, the Quebec public health law imposed fines of up to $200 or a jail term not to exceed three months. From 1919 on, the provincial law also stipulated a medical examination for persons found in houses of prostitution, which allowed the recorder to sentence infected women to a $100 fine.[61] Statistics compiled by the Montreal police indicate that many more women than men who were found in brothels were examined and that very few men were found officially to be infected.[62]

Experience with soldiers during World War One had proved that using condoms provided the best defence against disease. For reasons relating more to morals than to medicine, condom use, while fairly common elsewhere, was never officially endorsed in Quebec. In 1931, Rome went on official record as opposing lessons in "venereal prophylaxis" for young men in their two final years of college.[63] Hence the stress on an educational campaign based on fear and moral persuasion. The priests provided their parish halls for an anti-VD campaign centred on detection and continence. Practical prevention was not on the agenda and was seen only as a way of encouraging sin.

In 1917, a group of citizens formed the Committee of Sixteen "for the suppression, prevention and if possible the final extermination of commercialized vice."[64] During its eight years of existence, the Committee enlisted very few Francophones except for Father Henri Gauthier of the parish of Saint Jacques, situated in the red-light district. The committee conducted inquiries into the extent of vice in Montreal, especially the incidence of prostitution, sponsored lectures, acted as a pressure group on the municipal authorities, courts, and police to enforce the laws against bawdy houses, and inspired the provincial legislature to pass the 1920 law against the proprietors of these houses.[65] It helped get one chief of police fired and pressed the police to carry out raids in the red-light district. The members of the committee also asked for a police inquiry to be held, during which, primed by their own prior investigations, they provided invaluable evidence.[66] These social reformers, charged with progressive American ideology, banked on information and prevention to enforce a Christian morality that gave sexual morals pride of place.

As fashion and film were threatening morality, a number of different organizations appeared to regulate acceptable norms. In response to the appeal of Monsignor Bruchési, the Archbishop of Montreal, the Saint Vincent de Paul societies extended the League of Decency to the parish level. Other groups weighed in, like the Ligue des Femmes chrétiennes, founded in 1919 by former students of the Congregation of Notre Dame in response to "the indecency of modern fashions which are so deleterious to the morals of Christian youth."[67] The Anglophones of the MLCW had had a Committee on Moral Standards since 1913. In 1922 their counterparts in the FNSJB headed inquiries into particular subjects, such as the morality of theatres and cinemas and indecent fashions.[68] In Quebec, where censorship was reputed to be the most severe in the world, films previously subjected to the American censors then had to pass the provincial Bureau of Censorship and movie posters had to be approved by the Montreal police or, in Quebec City, by a citizen's committee.[69]

In 1927 the fire at the Laurier Palace, which killed seventy-eight children on a Sunday afternoon, took on the air of a divine punishment. It served as the pretext for a flurry of articles on the immorality of American movies, which were controlled by Jewish interests, as certain nationalist authors were quick to point out; by "de-Christianized Jewry," as Father Perrier put it in *L'Action française*.[70] Canon Harbour, author of ten articles on the subject, did not denounce the content of the films but the immorality of the darkened theatres where "temptations are the bait . . . and irreparable sins are lurking."[71] The Archbishop of Montreal, backed by every Catholic and nationalist association, called for an investigation into the Laurier Palace fire, not just into its causes but also into the morality of the cinema. On this last point, the report of the Royal Commission presided over by Judge Boyer concluded that "the movies are not, generally speaking, immoral."[72] But even if criticism of the immorality of the movies was not universal, the ecclesiastical condemnation from the pulpit touched the faithful during the weekly sermon.

During the entire period between the wars, the question of the movies never ceased to preoccupy not only the priests but also parish organizations and nationalist groups. In 1937, on the occasion of a Great Mission in October tied to the feast of Christ the King, the Catholic Film League launched a campaign in which the faithful would recite every week, with their hands raised, their promise "never to enter theatres where modesty and Christian morality are not respected."[73] For reasons of safety as well as morality, the theatres were closed to children under sixteen until 1960.

Censorship also extended to literature, and the Index of the Catholic Church acted as a guide to public libraries, which prohibited their subscribers from reading banned books. Authors who overstepped permissible limits learned a costly lesson. In 1934, Cardinal Villeneuve intervened to ban the novel *Les Demi-Civilisés* by Jean-Paul Harvey.[74] It was not that the subject matter was particularly improper, but the free love of a couple who wished their union to be "without contract or constraint" flew in the face of the model offered by polite society. Sacked from his post as editor-in-chief of the newspaper *Le Soleil,* Harvey paid dearly, not so much for his celebration of free love but more on account of his description of the social behaviour of the Quebec middle class. For that elite group, here was the material for scandal.

Society will nevertheless develop structures to foster the development of those virtues that will guarantee obedience to an ideal sexual code. Innocence, virginity, chastity, and monogamous heterosexuality within the institution of marriage will be assured only if the appropriate educational, reproving, and punitive agencies are fashioned. Thus the maternal instinct must be trained, and even more so the habit of sexual purity, the object of a constant struggle since the fall of Adam and Eve.

Primary sex education, based on poetic analogies to the birds and the bees, was acquired at home. Except in the country schoolhouses, the educational system reduced contact between the two sexes to a minimum. Absence of temptation was initially seen to offer the best protection, even if purity remained the thoroughgoing obsession of both teachers and preachers. By the end of the 1930s, the writings of Father Germain and, particularly, marriage preparation courses attempted to extend to a very limited group a certain degree of sex information. Ignorance was no longer believed to offer the most solid defence against the temptations of youth, but sex education remained the privilege of adults and those about to be married.

Those in contact with young female workers were agreed in saying that their ignorance exposed them to genuine dangers. In a world mined with obstacles, prevention presented a challenge that was met by various women's groups. Nuns and laywomen took the initiative in assisting young women who no longer lived at home by offering them lodging or organizing their leisure activities, all the time guiding their moral conduct. Even before the war, the Association catholique féminine had established the "Foyer," a boarding house for "the young woman who had to leave her family to earn her living in foreign parts," in this case, Montreal. During the war, which attracted an inexperienced female work force to the city as never before, the monthly bulletin of the Association published lists of boarding houses for the benefit of the young female worker.[75] The snares of the white slave trade remained a matter of concern, and in addition to its placement bureau and its reception centre, the Association was soon running a service in the train stations.[76] *Le Foyer* even printed advice for women travellers to spare them the "difficulties and dangers which lie in wait for the young woman left to her own devices."[77] Maria Rourke founded L'Aide à la Femme to extend aid to women and children in need of it and tried as well to organize a "train station mission," like that in France.[78] Finally, the FNSJB would form a committee for the protection of the young woman in 1938.[79]

Religious orders for a long time had concerned themselves with overseeing the virtue of young women. Especially in Montreal and Quebec City, a certain number of institutions were dedicated to the rescue and rehabilitation of those who were in danger of swelling the ranks of the delinquents, particularly prostitutes. In 1870, the Soeurs du Bon-Pasteur d'Angers founded Maison Sainte-Domitille at Laval-des-Rapides for the protection of girls and young women between the ages of six and sixteen. With a capacity of 650 students, this industrial school for orphans and abandoned children offered a primary and a commercial education. The youngest mothers who, after being delivered at the Hôpital de la Miséricorde, had nowhere to go were sent to Sainte-Domitille. After being referred by a judge, some 160 "delin-quent or simply endangered" young women could be accommodated at the Maison Sainte-Hélène, which was also run by the same order. Sher-brooke Street, in Montreal, was the site of their Refuge du Bon Pasteur, founded in 1844 and dedicated to the "protection and rehabilitation of the girl or woman who was in danger of falling or who had already fallen"; it could house some 300 women.[80]

In the years between the wars, the Hôpital de la Miséricorde of Montreal, founded in 1845 by Rosalie Cadron-Jetté at the suggestion of Bishop Bourget, received at least 560 unwed mothers a year. This Dorchester Street institution, like the one of the same name in Quebec City, answered several needs: it allowed for the concealment of a shameful sin, penance through work and pious exercises, rehabilita-tion, and, finally, the protection of society and the immediate family from the scandal caused by fallen women.[81]

Efforts to discourage deviant behaviour and rehabilitate delinquents were an integral part of the application of the ideals of sexual morality. The mission of protecting young girls, to which generations of women devoted themselves, tried to nip temptation in the bud, temptation that would lead to sexual experiences inevitably understood to have only catastrophic consequences. Control and watchfulness erected a fort-ress against unacceptable behaviour.

Female sexuality was barely acknowledged, and when it was, only in its most negative aspects. For women, sexuality was seen to have but one aim – motherhood. When she stepped outside these narrow limits, the woman of Quebec became the object of shame, ostracism, and occasional pity.

4

"Deviance"

Drawing a line inevitably defines a boundary; establishing a centre-point creates a periphery; pronouncing norms of behaviour produces deviation. In her book *L'Amour de la carte postale,* Madeleine Ouel-lette-Michalska analyses how difference is constructed through the power relations that allow for this particular form of cultural imperialism. [1] Norms and their deviations are the products of ideology and are laid down in a spatial and temporal context. Every woman, in whatever circumstance, who does not submit to the norm and who does not conform to prescribed modes of behaviour slips into social deviance. Before we consider the other side of maternity and sexuality, we should take a look at the function served by conduct that does not conform to the established rules.

Every piece of legislation, every regulation, is accompanied by the apparatus of surveillance and repression. Violations must be detected, for without the threat of punishment, there is a risk that the rules will lose their force. The evidence of certain mistakes would be plain enough: a pregnant young woman's body is a testament to sexual intercourse, whether she was a willing participant or not. Other forms of misconduct, like the use of contraceptives, for example, lend themselves more readily to concealment. In either case, the authorities attempted both to prevent the infraction and to detect it if prevention failed. For the Church, parish visits, confession, and moral instruction were also means of revealing not only those sins that had already been committed but the temptation to commit them as well, or the next occasion of sin. For laypersons, the mission of detection and prevention involved educational bodies, the social services, and even certain movements which encouraged informing. These included courses in home economics, the reception centres for young women newly arrived in the cities, and the anti-prostitution campaigns. The incidence

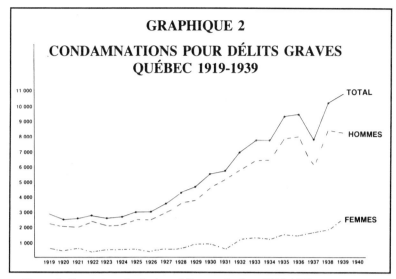

Figure 2. Convictions for Serious Offences, Quebec, 1919-1939
SOURCE: ASQ, 1920-40.

of deviant behaviour should reflect the effectiveness of all these instruments of control. In fact, since it is beyond our power to uncover each and every guilty soul, we cannot provide a final accounting of all the transgressions that presumably occurred.

Evidently, repression is never total. Total obedience cannot be guaranteed, owing to reasons related either to the nature of the demands themselves or to the presence and conviction of those agencies charged with enforcing them. If the principles no longer reflect social expectations, the theory and the practice will diverge, despite any mechanisms in place to keep them together. A gradual alteration in common values, what we might call the "evolution of morals," can often blunt the teeth of regulations that were elaborated to respond to social imperatives now becoming obsolete. If the population as a whole ceases to support the old commandments, there will be little enthusiasm to enforce them. Though respect for the outdated code may be lost, mental attitudes change so slowly that there are long periods of discordance before the rules are changed to conform with social expectations. It is then that the siren song of deviant behaviour is stronger than the call to perfection.

Even if values persist, behaviour goes hand in hand with economic conditions. The economic uncertainty of the early twenties and, later, the thirties caused a general apprehensiveness that could find expression in a heightened urge for conformity and in a renewed commitment to repress whatever threatened social cohesion. The same response to the threat of social upheaval at the end of the nineteenth century in Great Britain and the United States has been observed by other historians. This anxiety reveals itself in new efforts to contain all forms of social deviation, including everything involving sexuality.[2] Certain hardships, like unemployment, may produce contradictory effects. Juvenile delinquency may have declined during the Great Depression because of a greater parental presence in the home.[3] But this same unemployment seems to have given rise to an increased number of crimes against property.[4] Finally, a decrease in the birth rate and an increase in abortion would not be unrelated to hard times.

Behaviour is influenced not only by the times but also by the place. The effectiveness of social control is in part a function of community size. The rural parish, the village, the small town offer little scope for marginal activities. Large urban areas, on the other hand, make surveillance difficult. Conduct that overstepped the limits was most concentrated in cities of a certain size, such as Quebec City and Hull, but especially in Montreal. Urban dwellers, relatively more liberal than their country cousins, might be more tempted than they to transgress the prescribed codes of behaviour. Moreover, the metropolis, while providing services it could pretend to be unaware of, offered an asylum to women who wanted to disappear into the crowd. Those who wished to hide unusual sexual behaviour took refuge there, as did those who wanted to preserve their anonymity while seeking certain kinds of assistance. Unmarried mothers, lesbians, prostitutes, women seeking an abortion were gathered there in far greater numbers, relatively speaking, than anywhere else in Quebec. Montreal was the centre of deviant behaviour in the province and it is primarily from there that our examples are drawn.

Confronted by a wave of delinquent behaviour, the forces of order can either fortify repressive measures or yield to the obvious and to one degree or another shut their eyes to what is going on. Depending on what interests are involved in obeying the rules or are invested in illicit activity – here we are thinking, for example, of the conflicting interests of social reformers and the prostitutes' customers – either repression or toleration will prevail. The indifference of the authorities encourages moral decay and permits punitive measures to fall into abeyance. Agents of control, like the police, will prove insufficient to enforce the laws and regulations.

Since maintaining order depends on officers of the law, they must exist in sufficient numbers to be effective. But external circumstances have an influence on the size of the force. Other priorities, budgetary restrictions, and difficulties in recruitment all influence the availability of those who are charged with upholding the law. Toleration is not just the product of an impulse toward liberalization; it may also exist because repression is too expensive.

However broad the social consensus, the pronouncement of behavioural norms will be accompanied by the institution of sanctions. These are seen to profit both the individual and society as a whole. In a religious context, guilt might be expiated through penance that could assure the salvation of the soul. Attempts at rehabilitation might be added to these spiritual considerations. Institutions of reform that both punished and incarcerated provided the sinner the opportunity to make reparation for the sin and to embark on a new mode of life. The guilty could take advantage of their punishment to complete their education in every sense of the word, to learn to live according to established conventions.

Punishment is of value not just to the individual but to the whole community. It fulfils the injunction of "an eye for an eye, a tooth for a tooth." A vindictive society demands reparation. Reparation might take the material form of a fine, but more often it is a symbolic penalty that in no way compensates for the damage caused. Compensation remains inadequate and no one particularly cares, because the function of punishment is situated in a different area altogether.[5] In order to preserve the purity and cohesion of the social body, deviance has to be rooted out. Once rid of everything that interferes with its becoming what it wants to be, a community thinks to fulfil itself in unity, if not in homogeneity. If the deviants who undermine social harmony are not in fact eliminated, they are at least obscured so they do not appear as a blemish on the idealized communal self-portrait.

Isolation also serves to protect society from the example that might be set by the non-conformists. They must not become too familiar lest they inspire imitation. Scandalous women were to be relegated to the red-light districts, the hospitals, and the prisons to assure the innocence of their sisters. The psychiatrist Thomas Szasz once compared social deviance to contagious disease.[6] To prevent marginal behaviour from contaminating society, it had to be isolated. The disease model is especially pertinent to prostitution, which combined in the popular imagination the danger of physical contamination through the transmission of venereal disease with the danger of moral contamination through sexual looseness.

In addition, punishment has the function of deterrence. Recognition of the consequences of breaking the rules is essential to ensure that they are obeyed. The population is made aware of the limits of what is permitted.[7] Well-publicized penalties are reminders of what awaits the transgressor. In the old days, offenders were put in the stocks and the crowd admitted to public executions. In more recent times, we have come to count on subtler means to inform the public of the fate that lies in store for the delinquent. Accounts of criminal proceedings would be crammed with sordid descriptions; reporters would not omit a single detail when reporting a trial for infanticide or illegal abortion and would keep the public up to date on the number of police raids in the red-light districts. Although evil was to be isolated and hidden, punishment was to be publicized.

Female deviance was as specific as the norms that governed maternity and sexuality. There is no way that we can hope to deal with all the transgressions that occurred in Quebec in the period between the two world wars. If unpleasant consequences were to be avoided, violations of the norm had to be kept secret. We will remain with the most evident, identifiable, and recorded kinds of offence.

To refuse to be a mother emerged as the prime violation of the natalist code universally upheld by the religious and intellectual elite. This refusal could take one of four increasingly grave forms: contraception, abortion, child abandonment, or infanticide. We can only infer the incidence of contraception indirectly from demographic statistics, while noting that the frequency with which it was denounced suggests that its practice was expanding. Even more difficult is to discover the facts about the willingness to get rid of an unplanned pregnancy through abortion. The judicial archives will inform us about those whose lives are caught in their pages, the circumstances surrounding their deaths, and those from whom they sought help, but one is reluctant to generalize on the basis of so small a sample. Thus it is necessary to turn to qualitative sources, to discussions in which the most common defences are collected. Despite all these limitations, it is possible, by reading between the lines and by paying attention to gesture and sub-text, to get a picture of abortion during this period. Infanticide and child abandonment present the same difficulties, as they are the most carefully hidden of crimes and have neither witness nor proof.

Pregnancy was supposed to occur only within marriage. Supervision of young people, especially young women, the control over recreational activities, and the limitation on sex education were supposed to protect society against "illegitimate" births. Each year, however, around 2,500 children were born to "single mothers."[8] The great majority, one imagines, did not intend to become pregnant and some of them probably had not desired sexual intercourse. Whether they had consented to sex with the expectation of marriage or in the belief that they were protected from the consequences of intercourse, they all were labelled and treated as deviants. The registers, medical files, and correspondence preserved in the archives of the Hôpital de la Miséricorde constitute a mine of information about the daily experience of these women before and after delivery and about the attitudes of

Table 1
Female Criminality: Women Convicted
as a Percentage of Total Convictions

Year	Quebec	Canada
1918	27.94%	14.39%
1919	22.6	12.15
1920	18.06	9.35
1921	23.8	10.9
1922	13.7	10.2
1923	19.2	10.6
1924	19.3	11.2
1925	18.9	11.8
1926	18.5	11.8
1927	17.1	10.7
1928	15.9	10.4
1929	18.7	10.9
1930	16.1	9.9
1931	9.5	8.3
1932	18.1	10.2
1933	17.5	10.6
1934	16.1	9.9
1935	16.4	9.9
1936	15.4	9.4
1937	21.2	10.2
1938	18.3	9.6
1939	23.9	10.1

SOURCE: Canada, *Annual Reports on crime statistics,* 1918-1939.

families, religious authorities, and society toward those who became mothers without the benefit of holy matrimony.

Prostitutes earn their living by employing their sexuality with a number of partner-clients. Although their relationship with the clients is more of an economic than a sexual one, they were seen as sexual delinquents and we will include them here for that reason. Crimes committed by women constituted a much more considerable portion of total criminality in Quebec than elsewhere in Canada. The difference is explained by the role played by prostitution in Quebec, especially in Montreal, where it significantly inflated the number of crimes and infractions committed by women. Thus, in 1932, the peak year in the campaign against prostitution, 1,279 women were convicted, of whom

Table 2
Convictions of Keepers and Inmates of Bawdy Houses as a Percentage of Female Convictions, Quebec, 1928-1939

1928	61%	1934	76%
1929	66.3	1935	75.2
1930	57.8	1936	73.9
1931	44.5	1937	76.8
1932	82.9	1938	72.2
1933	81.9	1939	87

SOURCE: *ASQ*, 1929-1940.

1,061 were either madams or inmates of brothels.[9] Female crimes were primarily sexual.

Prostitution was only the most visible infraction of the sexual code of behaviour. Among sexual delinquents, one would have to include mistresses and kept women, difficult to distinguish at this distance, as well as divorced and remarried women, all of whom were associated with prostitutes in official denunciations. Prostitution would be approached therefore as a kind of ultimate deviance – extra-marital sex undertaken with no procreative intention, the antithesis of monogamy.

The sexual life, as we have seen, was to be confined to heterosexual relationships within marriage, practised either for reproduction or to relieve sexual tension. Masturbation remained excluded, if not eclipsed. As the prohibitions against solitary pleasure were very veiled, masturbation remained unacknowledged. Its very obscurity makes it impossible to study.

Then there are those practices situated outside the limits of heterosexuality. Lesbians do not even appear as a topic for public discussion and admonition. Hidden and discreet, they have left no written testimony. In her autobiography, the poet Elsa Gidlow mentions having met lesbians from Montreal sometime during the First World War, but she herself had to leave the city for New York before she had her first experiences with a woman.[10] The lesbian is the prime example of the sexual deviant: she spends her sexual life among those of her own sex, with no intention of either marrying or having children. It would require an oral history project to capture the lesbian reality of these decades among women who had so to conceal their preferences and their mode of life that they never developed a practice of communicating them at all.[11]

The non-conforming sexual behaviour that remains after these groups are dismissed centres on the refusal to become a mother, on unmarried motherhood, and on commercialized sex.

5

The Rejection of Motherhood

Sexuality could be detached from motherhood only within certain pre-determined limits or when such a separation could be justified by a higher set of ideals that would allow a departure from the prevailing standards of sexual behaviour. Not all women were able to conceive, and 16 per cent of those born in 1903 and aged between sixteen and thirty-six in the twenty years between the wars remained childless.[1] We presume that they did not choose their fate, since childless couples were generally regarded with pity. To repair the lack, they had recourse to crèches, orphanages, and parish priests in search of adoptive parents. For these couples, regardless of which partner was afflicted with sterility, it was rare that the woman had rejected maternity; rather, maternity had rejected her.

All agreed that a woman might sacrifice her procreative function in favour of an even more noble vocation. Members of religious orders enjoyed a privileged position in Quebec society, but the unmarried woman who remained "in the world" was in a rather more equivocal situation. The unmarried woman who devoted herself to her parents had her place in the family structure and it was accepted as well that some women simply never had a call from God. But most often the "old maid" was an object of pity. As was the case for her sisters in the convent, her piety redeemed her abdication of her reproductive role.

For a very great number of potential mothers, to reject conception or the baby itself did not mean the adoption of an alternative way of life; rather, it was a strategy dictated by circumstances and situated beyond the area accepted by those who defined the norms. Using contraceptives, terminating a pregnancy, abandoning a child at a nursery, indeed, even killing a newborn child were various means that merely comprised different degrees of choice beyond the limits of social expectation. Although there is an enormous difference between preventing

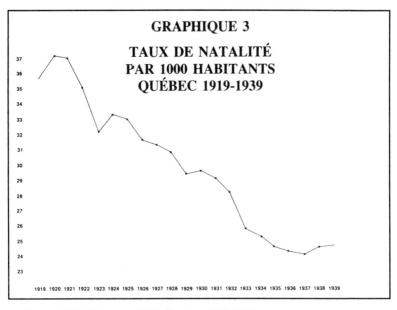

Figure 3. Birth Rate per 1,000, Quebec, 1919-1939
SOURCE: AC, 1920-1940.

conception and murdering a baby, both actions were located in the area of deviance and both were assimilated to one another in the natalist prescriptives of the Church. Contraception and abortion, construed as murder in the dominant discourse, remained exceptional if everpresent possibilities in the female reality.

Contraception

Contraception is a private practice and its use can only be estimated by observing the fluctuations in the birth rate by social class and over a period of time.

As Figure 3 indicates, Quebec was not completely untouched by the long decline in fertility that began in the 1880s. This decline was commonly attributed to industrialization and urbanization, although contraception and abortion had been known since at least the beginning of the nineteenth century.[2] Statistics show that, although the Quebec birth rate did not fall as quickly as it did in other provinces, each decade still registered a drop with the exception of the relatively prosperous years between 1901 and 1911. The fertility rate, that is, the number of births per thousand among women between the ages of fifteen and forty-nine, dropped from 180 to 155 between 1871 and 1921, a decline of 13.8

per cent, and this rate fell more precipitously thereafter, reaching 116 in 1931 and 102 in 1941, representing a decline of 25 per cent in the twenties and 12 per cent in the thirties.[3] This decline was not altogether the responsibility of the non-Catholic Anglophone population. Regional variations were pronounced, with fertility more restrained in the major cities than in the countryside, and different social classes demonstrated different demographic behaviour. The frequent denunciations issuing from the pulpit or from doctors' offices lead us to believe that certain more or less effective methods of contraception were in use, though, with the exception of *coitus interruptus,* these means were not easily come by.

Proponents of birth control attempted some forays into Quebec, motivated as much by humanitarian considerations as by the concern aroused in English Canada by the Quebec fertility rate. The Kitchener manufacturer and eugenicist A.R. Kaufman, who was devoted to the cause of birth control, underwrote family planning clinics in Toronto and Windsor as well as the distribution of birth control devices by mail or by social workers going from door to door. Far from being discouraged by the official attitude of the Roman Catholic Church, he extended his activities to Quebec in 1935. In 1936, the arrest of Dorothea Palmer, a nurse who worked for Kaufman in the Francophone area of Eastview in Ottawa, led to a notorious trial that ended in her acquittal. The court acknowledged that she was working *pro bono publico* – for the public good.[4] In this same year, Margaret Sanger forwarded to a Quebec woman the names of eight doctors, all with English-sounding surnames, who might be consulted on the subject – six were in Montreal, one in Lachine, and one in Huntingdon.[5] It is impossible to know how many Francophone women had recourse to their services, but one may presume that they were relatively few, came from the Montreal area, and likely lived in relatively comfortable circumstances.

A distinction must be made between contraceptive use on the part of young couples in their earliest encounters and by married couples who wished to plan their families. The latter were more likely to use contraception than were more impulsive and less cautious teenagers. The Ogino-Knauss method, reluctantly accepted by the Church for those married couples who knew how to plead their case, had to be well understood if it was to be in any way effective. Usually, another woman explained the monthly calculations, or a doctor, who might not be ready to share this information with an unmarried woman, would offer advice to married women. An unmarried woman would have to depend on explanations provided by her family or friends; even so, there was no guarantee that she could plan her sexual activities effectively using a method that relied on both discipline and the intimate co-operation of both partners. As for mechanical devices, few doctors would fit an unmarried woman with a diaphragm. Condoms, which were primarily associated with prostitution, could be bought at certain pharmacies or from illegal vendors,[6] but their use depended on male initiative. The sale of prophylactic devices, prohibited under article 207c of the Criminal Code until 1969, made owners of pharmacies liable to two years' imprisonment. Prosecutions of druggists occurred infrequently and this profession did not, in any case, have a monopoly on the sale of these products. Quacks also peddled pills that promised to "prevent a family." Those sold by the herbalist Alphonse Noël contained harmless amounts of rhubarb and quinine and were hardly effective.[7] In these circumstances, contraception for young unmarried persons would seem to be problematic and the birth rate among married women would appear to suggest a limited use.

Abortion

Whether she was married or single, a sexually active woman might very well experience an accidental pregnancy fraught with consequences. A considerable number attempted to solve their problem by trying to abort the fetus using methods ranging from the most harmless to the extremely dangerous. Abortion was part of the female reality, and despite all the taboos and anathemas, many women each year had recourse to abortion with greater or lesser impunity.

The case of Yvonne H. will serve to illustrate the worst that could happen to a woman who desperately tried to terminate her pregnancy. Yvonne H., fifteen-and-a-half years old, was brought to Saint Luc Hospital on May 14, 1934, suffering from serious abdominal pain. Her boyfriend, Émile, who was twenty-eight, had taken her two days previously to Delina Viau, who lived on the corner of Sherbrooke and Wolfe streets and had given Viau $35 to perform an abortion.

First Viau inserted tubing to dilate the cervix, followed by rubber catheters and pins, which she left in place for twelve hours. She kept Yvonne from Saturday till Monday, when complications set in. Viau called an Anglophone doctor, who advised her to take Yvonne home or to a hospital. Delina Viau and her sister-in-law brought Yvonne back home, and she was taken to hospital from there. She was in hospital for a week before she died, but not before making an *ante mortem* deposition before Sessions Court Justice Marin, the clerk of the court, certain lawyers, and a nurse, all of whom were present at her hospital bed. This sort of confession was absolutely essential in order to charge the person responsible for the abortion. It was all the more important because a deathbed statement required no corroboration.

The conversation proceeded as follows:

Q. Do you know that you are about to die?

A. Oh yes, oh yes, I know I'm going to die.

Q. Do you believe you are about to die?

A. Yes, I am very far gone. I can hardly speak; I haven't said a word this morning.

After eliciting this affirmation, the judge attempted to obtain the name and address of the abortionist as well as details about the procedure that had been followed. In this particular case, the patient did not die until three days later, which caused the defence lawyer to move that her testimony be excluded. Nevertheless, the judge allowed it, in view of the gravity of her condition. A search of Viau's premises followed and a bottle of veronal and some blood-spotted bedsheets were seized. She was arraigned on charges of murder and abortion, later changed to involuntary manslaughter, for which she was sentenced to a year's hard labour.

Yvonne H. was not very lucky. The operation had been carefully performed and the medical examiner found no marks around the cervix, but the infection introduced as a result of the procedure became generalized.[8] If this had not occurred, Yvonne would have taken her place among the hundreds of women every year who successfully terminated their pregnancies. Her experience was atypical only in its outcome, for the circumstances that brought her to Delina Viau were altogether ordinary.

Going for an abortion was only the final step in a process that ordinarily began with the first missed period. Almost every aborted woman who has left testimony admitted to first having tried mustard baths and gin, then powders, and finally some sort of implement.[9]

Nothing has ever demonstrated the worth of those mustard baths in which generations of anxious women have immersed themselves in the hope of bringing on their periods. A variety of vaginal douches might manage to terminate an unstable pregnancy. The most usual were based on bromo-quinine but permanganate of potassium (Lysol) was sometimes effective. The violence of whatever douche was used sometimes displaced the placenta and led to abortion; the antiseptic qualities of the liquid minimized the risk of infection. As for pills, those made of a parsley derivative could bring on a late period, but nothing more than that, and quinine pills, "the medication most frequently used by abortionists,"[10] according to medical examiner Dr. R. Fontaine, were only effective in the case of pregnancies already threatened. Ergot, the fungus long recognized as an abortifacient and relatively easy to obtain at the drugstore, was also taken, but it was commonly accompanied by the insertion of instruments.[11]

If the oral or vaginal use of these products did not bring about the desired effect, then one had to turn to various implements to dilate the cervix and rupture the sac to bring about the expulsion of the fetus. Slippery elm twigs, provided with a string, became mucilaginous in liquid and aided in the dilation of the cervix to permit a perforating instrument to be introduced. A metal loop might serve this purpose, mounted in a rubber catheter and left in the uterus until its contents were expelled.[12] This was the most popular method of the time. There were decided risks to this procedure and the operation demanded a dexterity born of experience. Clumsiness could result in a perforated uterus or peritonitis, both commonly fatal.

The fate of Yvonne H. was unusual; we cannot depend on the statistics of deaths following botched abortions to arrive at some idea of how frequently the operation was performed. Actually, the majority of the men and women performing abortions knew what they were doing and not all infections ended in death. Furthermore, medical records often hid the cause of death under these circumstances – the classic explanation for vaginal hemorrhage was a fall down a staircase. These falls, accidents, and voluntary exhaustion cannot be evaluated. What are we to make of the story of a woman who was pregnant five times between the ages of eighteen and twenty-five? Three of these pregnancies ended in a Caesarian section and two in stillbirth. For her sixth pregnancy, the clinic at Notre Dame Hospital told her to come into hospital the moment she went into labour. She felt the first contractions at noon, but she was in the middle of moving. She continued her activities until 8:00 p.m., when she was delivered of a stillborn infant by Caesarian section.[13]

Commentary of the period is rife with observations about abortion. The tirades of the Church, speeches from the bench, and medical denunciations indicate that abortion was a commonplace event. A lawyer sitting on the Coderre Commission mentioned twenty-five houses on St. Denis Street between Craig and Roy where illegal operations, as they were euphemistically termed, could be obtained.[14] Judges routinely denounced these offences in their speeches to the jury. For example, Judge Letellier of Trois-Rivières in 1923 and Judge Wilson of Montreal in 1925, both having heard trials of doctors accused of producing an abortion, were of the opinion that this was a far too frequent practice. Two years later, Judge Wilson remarked that these trials were becoming more numerous, which suggests that abortion was becoming more frequent.[15]

Premises billing themselves as private medical clinics, common in the period, offered services to women whose numbers are difficult to determine because these private establishments were extremely and necessarily discreet. Physicians were aware of what was going on in them. In an article published in 1922, Dr. O.A. Cannon presented the results of his study of fifty-one women he investigated following abortion or miscarriage. Of this number, twenty-two admitted to having brought about the abortion. The doctor added that this 43 per cent would have been considerably higher had every woman been equally frank.[16] If the doctors are to be believed, the economic constraints of the depression years produced an upsurge in the rate of illegal operations. In 1933, Dr. Léon Gérin-Lajoie of Notre Dame Hospital observed that there seemed to have been a marked increase in the number of induced abortions, at least among patients brought in to the gynecological wards. He added that on a particular day, eleven of the eighteen beds on this service were occupied by women following induced abortion.[17]

Court cases give no real idea of the number of illegal operations, since these records relate only to those abortions that resulted in medical complications and, commonly, death. The annual federal crime statistics record seventy-seven charges of illegal abortion in Quebec between 1919 and 1939, of which fifty-five ended in conviction.[18] Between 1931 and 1939, the Montreal police received thirty-nine complaints of abortion and only proceeded to arrest in seven cases. Each year, the number of attempted abortions reported to the authorities was higher – there were twenty-six in 1931, for example – but these were much more difficult to prove.[19] The imprecision of these data makes them impossible to quantify. The municipal and provincial police received complaints that led in certain cases to police raids and sometimes to arrests, almost all of which were concentrated in Montreal.

Physicians who were called on to treat the consequences of the operation give the impression that abortion was hardly a rare event. The doctor-narrator of *Soeur ou fiancée,* Dr. René de Cotret, complains of how often his patients request abortions.[20] The novel, published in 1932, is set at the turn of the century and, like the rest of this author's work, draws heavily on his own experiences. In *La Chair décevante,* by Jovette Bernier, the father of the prospective child brutally says, "Kill it!"[21] Even when it was rejected as an option, abortion remained a possibility for women in trouble.

Doctors turned less often to fiction than to their professional journals or to opinion pieces to voice their opposition to the termination of pregnancies. Dr. Cannon used the pages of the *Canadian Medical Association Journal* to denounce abortionists and to demand that the sale of catheters, ergot, and other abortifacients be prohibited in drugstores and that pharmacists be required to cut slippery elm, which could also be used to make a tonic, into small pieces before placing it on sale.[22] Products capable of bringing on a period or expelling a fetus remained available to customers who wanted them. Physicians continued to denounce abortion, but its practice did not diminish. Dr. Ernest Couture, author of the popular manual *La Mère canadienne et son enfant,* which was distributed by the Department of Health, remarked, "These days, there is an inclination to view this practice with too much indulgence."[23]

The incidence of puerperal septicemia reported by the provincial Heath Service gives indirect evidence of the morbidity and mortality that may be attributed to abortion. A certain proportion of reported cases, estimated at 17 per cent in the 1930s, was due to induced abortion, while the rest followed childbirth or spontaneous abortion.[24] In 1932, however, the health officer's report was more specific and noted that out of forty-four cases of septicemia, two were occasioned by "self-induced abortion," while twenty-eight, that is, 64 per cent, were the consequence of other abortions.[25] The majority were associated with voluntary interventions, but it is impossible to establish the ratio of induced abortion to the total number of childbirths and spontaneous miscarriage. Nevertheless, these reports always underestimate the actual numbers and, in order to preserve family pride, overlook the number of septic abortions passed off as peritonitis cases by an understanding physician. Carelessness coupled with the connivance of doctors more often than not assured a discretion that falsified the statistics.

The description of premises visited by the police suggests a constant coming and going. There were genuine clinics whose beds were rarely empty. Herbalist Alphonse Noël maintained an "operating theatre" on St. Catherine Street that employed the services of a nurse trained by the Hôpital de la Miséricorde.[26] In Collin Lane, the police found one double and three single beds used by Gabrielle Lachapelle's patients, while on Amherst Street Simone Leclerc would deal with five or six women at a time, sometimes two to a bed.[27] A judge spoke quite correctly of "professionals who earn their living by engaging in this profession."[28] Women who required such services appear to have had no difficulty finding out where to go – one might get an address from the druggist; another would look for the name of a so-called doctor in the telephone directory; others might be told by their parents, friends, or lovers.[29]

Abortion was therefore relatively available for around $25, which represented at least a week's wages for a female worker, even more for a domestic. If the average cost of an abortion was $25, then some would pay only $20 or even $15, while others might have to go to $35. One married woman paid $200 for a doctor.[30] A seventeen-year-old young woman who was on relief pledged her watch at Aux Trois Boules, a pawn shop on Craig Street, for which she got $5 to put toward the cost of an abortion.[31] In order to pay for his services, a prostitute was forced to have sexual relations with her herbalist-abortionist.[32]

The great majority of women recuperated after a period of pain and suffering that must not be underestimated. The success rate explains the number of repeaters. Most women did not feel they were running any great risk. In order to reassure one of her patients, Rose L. Deschamps boasted of having "fixed up" her servant four times. [33] Certain women used abortion in place of contraception. A mother of four, separated from her husband, who had already undergone an abortion by curettage, had another the following year in which the abortionist used pins. In the opinion of her doctor, "The patient has made a good recovery from these operations and remains in excellent health." [34] Two years later, having resorted to the usual mustard baths, she had catheters inserted with fatal results – it was an ectopic pregnancy. But such a pregnancy was unusual; the greatest threats lay in perforation of the uterus or infection due to uncleanliness.

If an infection did develop and the patient was taken to hospital in time, she might expect to recover in a matter of weeks. Of course, a certain number did die of general peritonitis following an induced abortion, and it was then that the hospital called in the police. Only in these circumstances has testimony been left concerning the procedures followed that led to an arrest. No possible means were neglected to obtain an *ante mortem* deposition. When Jeanne M., twenty, who died of jaundice, general peritonitis, and infection of the uterus at Saint Luc Hospital, begged to be left alone, the nurse gave her an injection and told her that she would rest afterwards. Her testimony led to the arrest and sentencing of her abortionist, a day labourer, to two years less a day in prison for involuntary manslaughter. [35]

Barring a disaster, abortionists could operate for years with impunity. Even when they were tried, more often than not they were acquitted. According to the Federal Bureau of Statistics, fifty-eight persons (eighteen women, forty men) charged with abortion were sentenced between 1919 and 1939. Between 1929 and 1939, out of the fourteen men and ten women charged in twenty-four cases drawn from the Montreal judicial archives, ten – four men and six women – were found guilty, usually for involuntary manslaughter. Most of those convicted were repeat offenders. Sentences ranged from fifteen months to fifteen years, but only four received sentences of five years or more for murder. [36] It was very difficult to prove that the procedure had not been initiated by someone else or by the patient herself before she arrived at the clinic. The objects seized – cannulas, slippery elm twigs, and medications – could easily be for personal use, as L. Bélec maintained to the court's satisfaction. [37] Finally, the operation itself left little incriminating evidence behind, and doctors often declared themselves unable to determine what procedure had been followed. [38]

The difficulty of establishing proof and producing witnesses partly explains the infrequency of trials for abortion. For abortionists, the procedure appears to have offered relatively few risks in return for significant revenue in a period of economic crisis, which seems to have made abortion a growth industry. The statistics, which reflect police activity as much as the frequency of offences, indicate a marked increase in 1931, with peaks in 1936 and again in 1939. As we have already seen, this increase is corroborated by the observations of hospital physicians.

Depending on their training, their social class, and their gender, the men and women who chose to offer this kind of service came to it via different routes. Of the twenty-four charged between 1929 and 1939, four male abortionists had gone to medical school and, of these, two had been stricken off the medical register. According to their patients, several other practitioners also claimed to be doctors. Of ten women who were charged, two were registered nurses and one was a midwife in Quebec City. The others had no particular training, though they had been offering their services for some time. Three of the accused had records – for one, it was his third trial for murder, abortion, or involuntary manslaughter; for another, it was his fifth.[39]

Those who performed abortions on a certain scale were primarily motivated by greed. They might distance themselves altogether from their patients, sending them home with the advice to "jump" to encourage the expulsion of the fetus and refusing to heed their pleas if the pains persisted or a hemorrhage occurred. Other women, in contrast, would keep their patients in bed in their apartments and, when necessary, call a co-operative doctor or arrange transport to a hospital. There were undeniable risks, but even when a death occurred they would be arrested only following an incriminating declaration.

An examination of thirty medical and judicial files for the period 1925-39 in the Montreal area provides a very incomplete picture of abortion in Quebec. If the files give us some idea of the abortionists who were operating between the wars, it is still, except for the few cases already described, extremely difficult to construct a picture of the women who resorted to abortion during this period. These files deal only with hospital cases, of which half ended in death. The victims of these tragedies had certain factors in common – they were quite young, on average, four them being only fifteen or sixteen years old and the oldest thirty-two. The majority acted promptly – six of them were ten weeks pregnant or less, but four were in their fifth month. More than one confessed to having previously tried to terminate a pregnancy or to having been successful in producing an abortion.

Three-quarters of those about whom we have information were unmarried. We may not conclude from this fact that these women had looser morals or were more inclined to resort to abortion than married women. We should be cautious about drawing such conclusions from so small a sample. It is possible that married women were successful in producing their own abortions and recovered as well as they could to pursue their normal household duties. They were probably more numerous than the statistics suggest because the assistance of relatives or friends was often more reliable than the aid of those who specialized in illegal operations. In any event, such assistance certainly cost less.[40]

Almost all of the unmarried women involved in these court cases worked as domestics. Is it coincidental that practically every woman who came in contact with the authorities was from the working class? How can we explain that no middle-class woman was subjected to an *ante mortem* deposition or, indeed, figured at all in any trial during the entire period under study? Without departing too far from established fact, we can offer certain hypotheses. A well-informed woman, one able to pay the cost, could turn to a medical specialist who promised the best sanitary conditions and post-operative care. Through their social connections, certain women could consult a relative or a sympathetic medical friend. Though they do not wish to be quoted, women of this period recall certain doctors who performed abortions for decades without apparently ever being bothered by the authorities. They were not numerous, since gynecologists and even general practitioners did not usually need to supplement their incomes with this sort of practice. During the Great Depression, physicians experienced some difficulty collecting their fees. Some of them might, perhaps, have gone in for an illegal practice in order to maintain their standard of living. It is more probable, however, that some medical abortionists needed extra money to support a drug habit and that others only dealt with those who were close to them. The records of doctors accused of abortion commonly reveal prior convictions linked to narcotics use or trafficking. In addition to any self-serving motivations, one cannot exclude humanitarian concerns on the part of certain doctors who were able to dispense services to women in desperate need of them.

It was more common for a woman who was informed to obtain a therapeutic dilation and curettage from her doctor in the earliest stages of pregnancy. One could always pretend to be ignorant of one's condition. Then there was therapeutic abortion in non-Catholic hospitals when the life of the mother was in danger; although forbidden by Catholic dogma, it constituted the solution of choice for those who could consult a co-operative physician. Since 1892, Canadian law had permitted an intervention that caused the death of the fetus in order to save the life of the mother either before or during delivery.[41] The medical literature of the time contains a discussion of the cases and the causes that justify such interventions. Tuberculosis was one of the conditions in which abortion might be part of the treatment at the time.[42] In

Quebec, which had the highest rate of tuberculosis in Canada, it is very likely that it would constitute a sufficient justification, at least in non-denominational hospitals.

Middle-class women were likely to be healthier and better fed than their poorer sisters, which would make them better able to recover rapidly from the effects of such an operation and to combat infection. Young domestic workers did not enjoy this advantage. Normande D., seventeen, who was on relief, is described in the autopsy report as being "extremely thin." Ida L., sixteen, a servant from St. Donat, was also "thin and weak of constitution." The same was observed of Jeanne M., a twenty-year-old domestic worker who died of generalized peritonitis.[43] These were the kinds of women who would have spent the night two or three to a bed in the abortionist's flat and then returned to their own unhealthy rooms to recuperate. The women who employed these domestics would have had an altogether different experience in a hospital, in a private clinic, or in the comfort of their own homes. If they were unable to obtain the services of a co-operative doctor or if they wished to assure absolute secrecy about their condition, women who knew where to go could travel south of the border where, on the pretext of a shopping trip perhaps, they could arrange matters satisfactorily, with no one at home the wiser.

A healthier environment and more competent medical services nevertheless could not provide an absolute guarantee against fatality. We may presume that the middle class had the means to hush embarrassing situations. Peritonitis might have several causes and might well be used to disguise something quite different. That no woman of the leisure class appears in the fifteen years of cases we examined may be explained by their more favourable circumstances, their access to more reliable services, the greater discretion to which their families could avail themselves. There is nothing to indicate – and it seems highly unlikely – that abortion did not occur among the middle and upper classes.

In comparison to the unyielding official line, we see that in practice behaviour was far freer than the public sanctions might have led us to expect. That motherhood, which was so commonly glorified, could be consciously rejected runs counter to established dictates on the social order in general and on women in particular. Not only did a group of women whose numbers were surely far larger than we can establish defy the taboos, the diktats, and the excommunications, but they generally did so with impunity. It is true that the attitudes expressed toward those dying women from whom confessions were extracted were unyielding and contemptuous, but on the other hand, before they wound up in the hospital, these women had managed to find a way to put an end to a pregnancy they did not want. They had been able to find abortionists without too much difficulty. If those addresses were known to them, they must have been known to the police as well. Nevertheless, in an entire decade, only two actions originating with the police have come to light, one in 1929, the other in 1937.

The medical profession had a vested interest in getting rid of quacks, doctors who were practising after losing their licences and amateurs who were engaging in a medical procedure. In both the United States and Canada, doctors had played an important role in the criminalization of abortion in the nineteenth century. The attack on abortionists was part and parcel of the movement for the professionalization of medicine and the elimination of all manner of rivals – chiropractors, midwives, homeopaths, and traditional healers.[44] The College of Physicians in Quebec demanded greater rigour from the police, but we have only come across two cases in which the police initiated a search of the premises of a known abortionist.

In 1937, the College of Physicians hired a man and a woman who was to pretend to be pregnant to consult Gaston Deniger, a chauffeur by profession. Deniger gave them a bottle of pills, which the woman subsequently gave to the College, and offered her an injection that would provoke the expulsion of the fetus. When the police were informed they searched the premises, seizing instruments and the usual medications that could be used as evidence. This time the proceeding, which was begun by the prestigious College of Physicians, was successful – Deniger pleaded guilty and got a month in jail at hard labour and a fine of $100.[45] The sentence was probably not sufficient to discourage him from resuming his activities at a later date.

The police did not bother abortion clinics – their indifference the result of their reluctance to view the act as criminal or a sign that they tolerated a service to which they themselves might have recourse. For centuries the abortion of a fetus before "quickening," that is, in the first trimester, had been considered neither crime nor sin. In 1803 the British Parliament passed a law that would become a model for Canadian legislation. For the first time the voluntary destruction of the fetus became a criminal act, whether or not movement was felt, though the punishment was less in the latter case. Following Confederation this distinction was erased, and the mother, as well as the abortionist, was made liable for a maximum sentence of imprisonment for life.[46] The laws making abortion in the first trimester a crime and inculpating the pregnant woman had been passed within living memory. Women saw it as more a matter of bringing on their periods than of destroying a life that did not appear to them yet to exist. Once again, René de Cotret, in his *Soeur ou fiancée,* captures the thinking of the period very well when he has his newly pregnant heroine sincerely believe that "it isn't life yet."[47] It is hardly surprising that the Church felt regularly moved to remind the faithful of the gravity of the sin.

Women who terminated their pregnancies had long gone unpunished. The change in the law hardly disturbed traditional toleration. No mother was found guilty for having procured the abortion of a non-viable fetus, no matter what means she used. One can understand why the authorities might have been reluctant to pursue the dying women who made their *ante mortem* depositions, but it was well known that hospital beds were also occupied by women recuperating in the aftermath of an abortion, and no one initiated prosecutions against these patients. They were not, however, innocent bystanders, since they had taken the initiative to seek out an abortionist, who, after all, did not solicit customers and who did not advertise. It was evidently far more important to eliminate the doctors' competition, those who were performing illegal operations, especially those about whom there was evidence that they were placing their patients' lives in danger.[48]

The consequences of what was termed an illegitimate birth were so serious that the women who violated the prohibitions in order to escape them sometimes elicited considerable sympathy. No one was unaware of the shame that was heaped upon the unwed mother or the difficulties she would face taking care of the baby once it was born. People could recognize that the woman with child and without a husband might very well have recourse to the most extreme means to rid herself of her sin and its consequences.

It had to be admitted that, regardless of the strength of the prohibitions, there would always be those who did not conform and that society had, secretly, to accommodate itself to them. Despite all the pious declarations on the subject of chastity, what family was proof against accident? Despite the public celebration of the large family, how many wives, whose ambitions in this direction had been exceeded several times over, might not beg for a termination? Underneath the public intransigence lay a more tolerant practice that acted as a safety valve for the most desperate cases. A great number of women would no doubt be unable to take advantage of it – religious scruples, ignorance, isolation, or simple lack of initiative prevented them from taking steps in time to remedy their situation. Some of these, faced at last with the undeniable evidence of a pregnancy come to term, rejected motherhood in a fatal way.

Infanticide

Every year the newspapers carried several reports of the discovery of the bodies of newborn infants and, occasionally, of the prosecution of women for infanticide. Some desperate mothers, incapable of facing their accidental pregnancies until too late or unable to find an abortion, always had done away with their children at birth. If the pregnancy had been well enough disguised, the death of the newborn might be hidden successfully. In order to prevent such disappearances, since the fifteenth century French law had required unmarried pregnant women to declare their condition, and from the eighteenth century onwards, British law, subsequently adopted by the North American colonies, forbade the disguising of a pregnancy.[49] This prohibition appeared again in article 272 of the Criminal Code of Canada, which made it illegal for:

> anyone to dispose of the dead body of any child in any manner whatsoever, with the intent to conceal the fact that the mother was delivered of it whether the child died before, or during, or after childbirth.

In the twentieth century, the provinces made the registering of births mandatory. In 1930, a bulletin from the Montreal Health Service reminded the public that, beginning with the month of March, births must be registered within four months or a fine of $50 would be imposed.[50] Despite all these efforts to control and discourage infanticide, it remained among the most secret of acts, accomplished in an isolation even greater than that for abortion.

We cannot judge how widespread this practice was by counting how often dead babies were reported found and even less by tallying the numbers of women accused of infanticide. It was not uncommon in the nineteenth century and before; it was perhaps less frequent in the twentieth century but had certainly not disappeared.[51] Although the police only reported one or two prosecutions for infanticide each year, the coroner found a number of deaths were "due to criminal negligence in the birth of a child." In this connection, in 1922 the court reported that the situation in Montreal was improving, since only nine infant deaths resulting from criminal negligence had occurred that year.[52] This improvement may have been due to the upturn in the economy, which had sagged after the Great War, since the depression in the thirties would be accompanied by an increase in tragedies of this kind. The Montreal daily *La Presse* reported in March, 1931, that "a second newborn infant had been found dead this week."[53] How many of these discoveries were not reported in the papers and how many were never discovered at all?

Four trials for infanticide allow us to draw some impression of the motives and circumstances that led to the act. In 1931, Juliette S. was accused of "illegally causing the death of her newborn child by strangling it with a cord, thus committing murder." According to police evidence, she had given birth by herself under the stone steps of the old Montreal aqueduct on Atwater. The body, wrapped in a coat, was found the next morning in an alley. It was not hard for the court to sympathize with Juliette S. Married at sixteen and separated for the past five years, she already had several children her mother was looking after and she was living in a furnished room with the father of the child, a carter. Six weeks earlier she had lodged a complaint with the police after her husband had beaten her up. According to her sister, she also suffered from epileptic seizures. Judge Charles Wilson, in his address to the jury, tried to save her from a murder sentence. He reminded the jury that it had not been proved that the child was a human being, the necessary prerequisite to a charge of murder. To be a human being, it must have completely emerged from its mother's womb and it was not certain that it had been fully born at the time of strangulation. In the case of such profound uncertainty, the benefit of the doubt must be given to the accused, and this is indeed what the jury did.[54]

The circumstances of Jeannette B., a servant on a farm in Montcalm County, were no less pathetic. After giving birth by herself in her room, she wrapped her apron around the neck and body of the baby, which she then hid in the cellar. She was found guilty but was sentenced only to the time already served, some nineteen months.[55]

Another unwed mother, twenty-seven, was sentenced to two years in jail following her arrest for stabbing her twins "because they were crying and . . . her parents might find out about them."[56] In each case, it was an unmarried mother who found the arrival of the child a catastrophe. They were poor and ill-educated, incapable of denying their crime in the face of the evidence and unable to enlist the services of a reputable lawyer. They confessed their crime and received light sentences, considering the gravity of the offence they had been charged with. Juries were sympathetic, as these women did not constitute a public danger and were unlikely to do it again. They had become pregnant unintentionally and were faced with a situation they could not cope with.

The courts evinced little concern for the victims of infanticide. It was not so much a question of guilt being diminished because the child, having lived so briefly, counted for less than an adult or because it was destined to a harsh life. Rather, the situation of the mother was the primary factor, and we find this a consideration even when it was a matter of the murder of a two-month-old child. Hélène V., a thirty-year-old private nurse, had boarded her child out from its birth while she worked in a home in Montreal. Because she could no longer pay the nursery to which she owed $7.50 for two weeks' board, she was told to come and pick up the baby. Late at night, during a snowstorm, she put him down among the trees on the side of Mount Royal, where his body was found in the spring. She refused to plead guilty – there were no witnesses, and, even though she had been seen with the baby shortly before midnight and without him shortly afterwards, the jury found her not guilty.[57]

Child Abandonment

There were various ways to get rid of a child the mother could not take care of. "I am forced to abandon him because I cannot provide for him. He has not been baptized," read the note pinned to the baby found by the sacristan of the Église du Gésu during the hard winter of 1923. The police brought him to the Grey Nuns' crèche where he joined the other abandoned babies. The daily newspaper *La Patrie* printed an editorial that was very sympathetic toward the mother and critical of a society that forced a woman to abandon her child in this way.[58] This kind of incident regularly turned up in the daily papers; ten years later, for example, a brief news item in *Le Canada* reported that a woman asked the family next door "to adopt her child." When she was refused, she threw herself into a quarry where she was later found buried with her baby.[59] Once again, this tragedy aroused sympathy rather than horror or condemnation.

Such stories, which could have been lifted from the pages of popular fiction of the nineteenth century, were by no means rare. Each year, lost children were brought to the Montreal police. They would never be claimed and had to be placed in orphanages. There were forty-seven such cases in 1928; the number rose to 107 in 1929 and would vary between a high of sixty-eight and a low of nine throughout the 1930s. The mystery surrounding their origins was never solved. Thus, in 1932, the municipal police received fifty-two complaints of child abandonment; ten persons were arrested and sixty-eight children had to be placed in orphanages.[60]

In addition to the large crèches run by the Grey Nuns and the Miséricorde Sisters, Montreal had a number of nurseries that were often associated with the private hospitals on St. Denis and Mount Royal. In 1922, sixty-nine houses boarded between 250 and 275 children at the expense of the municipal authorities. A nurse inspected them monthly and submitted her report to the Montreal Health Service.[61] The nurseries provided a service for single mothers and widows who had to work and who were in a position to pay fees running between $1.60 a week up to $15 a month during the 1930s.[62] Arrears rapidly accumulated, visits came further and further apart, and soon the nurseries had to deal with the problem of children who were not picked up. "I have two children boarding with me who will be put up for adoption if they are not called for within three days," wrote a Madame Bouchard under the heading "Adoptions" in the classified ads in *La Presse* in 1930.[63] There seems to have been an active traffic for some years, with nurseries providing babies between the ages of two weeks and ten months. The mothers who left their children in this way probably intended to keep them but, unable to pay the fees, had to resign themselves to a new home being found for them, which they hoped would be warm and prosperous.

These immense crèches and orphanages and the numerous day nurseries were witness to the need to care for hundreds of children whose mothers simply could not provide for them. The monthly inspections did not prevent a certain number of abuses, such as the one we catch a glimpse of involving the proprietor of a private clinic and nursery on St. Denis Street. During the night of April 19, when the temperature was 0° Celsius, an unknown person left five children under the age of two outside the door of a hospice in Trois-Rivières; during the night of May 10, six more; on May 20, another five; and on June 13, a final four. On May 10, six babies were left at the Ouvroir in St. Hyacinthe, followed by two more on June 14 and July 10. During the night of June 22, four babies were abandoned on the staircase of an institution in Granby. Suspicion came to rest on a Madame H. Dorion, née Elphégina Fontaine, a forty-five-year-old nurse who was accused of having abandoned a total of twenty-eight tiny babies between April and June. These babies had been placed with her by their mothers for adoption. It was a lucrative business during a depression since the women had to pay $50 to defray the costs of care pending adoption. With the aid of her daughters, who were not charged, Madame Dorion disposed of her charges, for whom she probably could not find so many adoptive families, by simply leaving them. Before the jury rendered a verdict, Elphégina Dorion died in jail.[64] Her trade gives a glimpse of the practice known in English-speaking countries as "baby farming." It is once more impossible to estimate how widespread this kind of thing was; what it does demonstrate, however, is that for a considerable number of mothers, the solution to an unacceptable pregnancy was adoption into a family able to care for the child.[65]

About 20 per cent of Quebec single mothers gave birth at the Hôpital de la Miséricorde in Montreal. It is here we must look to examine what options were offered to those women who had brought an undesired pregnancy to term. Despite expert advice, which recommended that mothers keep their babies, only 14.6 per cent of Miséricorde patients left the hospital with their babies in their arms.[66] The majority left their babies at the hospital crèche, after having paid $50 to "abandon" them and to pay for their upkeep prior to adoption. Unburdened of the child who would serve as a constant reminder of her sin, the woman might hope to embark on a new life without being pursued by the souvenir of a mistake that would be a source of shame and cause for ostracism from respectable society.

Those who hoped to be able to care for their child some day and who undertook to pay a dollar a week for its care, left it at the crèche but had permission to visit it once a month. A number of these women intended to recover their children when their economic situation improved or if they married. These separations were often extremely painful, according to the letters between former patients of the hospital and the sisters who were taking care of their children. Some mothers sent money to receive photographs of their children; one, noticing that her child's legs were bowed, paid for corrective shoes. They worried about the care the boarders received: "Make sure she goes outside. I want her to be healthy."[67] They paid the boarding fee regularly for months, sometimes for years, but little by little the payments became less frequent until all contact was finally broken and the child, if he or she was still alive, became a candidate for adoption. The abandonment of all these children in the crèches or nurseries marked the failure of those who had hoped to sort things out and who finally had to give up in the face of the social and economic demands of their daily lives.

Motherhood was an ideal that fulfilled itself in privileged surroundings – in a family consisting of two married parents with a decent standard of living, a place to live, and a job for at least one of the partners. If these conditions were missing, the arrival of a child could only be viewed as a catastrophe. For a domestic servant, a child meant the loss of her position and an economic burden. A woman in this situation had mortgaged her future, made herself unmarriageable, and become an object of scandal. Even for the married woman, who perhaps had more frequent recourse to abortion than her single counterpart,[68] an excess pregnancy often represented an emotional and economic burden it was impossible to assume. An examination of the registers of Quebec orphanages reveals that the majority of children placed there had both parents living and that a significant percentage had one.[69] Even if these institutions often acted as emergency centres for stays of less than three months, certain children remained there, more or less abandoned, for years, in order to allow their parents, typically the mothers who had responsibility for them, to survive.

Up to a certain point, the authorities were aware of the fate of women whose lives were suddenly turned upside-down by a biological accident. Even if the censors believed they were properly punished for having exercised their sexuality outside the confines fixed by morality, the courts were merciful and officers of the law did not go out of their way to arrest condom sellers or abortionists. The consequences of an unplanned pregnancy were so serious that no amount of preaching could put an end to practices that expressed a rejection of the child either at conception, during pregnancy, or after birth itself.

6

Wages of Sin: Unwed Mothers

Premarital sex and the birth of a fatherless, hence nameless, child threatened to overturn the patriarchal family, a cornerstone of Quebec society. An irregular pregnancy of this sort was proof positive of the failure to guard one's daughters and evidence of their freedom in an area where they were not supposed to be free. It created a drama in which the actresses were not permitted a role in the family play. It furthermore made all too evident a lapse that might otherwise have passed unnoticed. Only if every trace of the transgression were erased could the sinner be reintegrated into her normal society. The women who were either unable or unwilling to obliterate the consequences of their sexual activity, activity to which they may or may not have consented, entered the ranks of those who had long been termed unwed mothers.

There are no exact data on the frequency of extramarital pregnancy, but it must have been far more common than the figures indicate, if one considers how often abortion or miscarriage must have intervened before a pregnancy was brought to term. The "illegitimate" birth rate in Quebec ranged between .03 and .07 per cent, less than the national average and lower than that in most Western countries. According to official statistics, which probably underestimate the facts, 2.9 to 3.4 per cent of live births were to unwed mothers.[1] Close to 40 per cent of these births took place at either the Hôpital de la Miséricorde in Montreal or the one in Quebec City, 560 a year on average in Montreal and 457 in Quebec.[2] Some women who were rather more fortunate gave birth in private maternity clinics, typically far away from home, or at the home of distant relatives or, more unusually, under the familial roof, which had often hidden the young woman's condition for a number of months. The women who gave birth at the two Miséricorde hospitals comprise a group quite representative of the majority of unmarried

Table 3
Illegitimate Births, Quebec, 1926-1939

1926	2,055	1933	2,433
1927	2,319	1934	2,335
1928	2,419	1935	2,506
1929	2,359	1936	2,469
1930	2,519	1937	2,451
1931	2,450	1938	2,525
1932	2,433	1939	2,668

SOURCE: Quebec, Annual Report of the Minister of Health and Welfare, 1927-1940.

mothers and, thanks to the archives and medical files, one that is easier to analyse.

The Hôpital de la Miséricorde had been performing a service for single mothers and "illegitimate" children since the mid-nineteenth century. In 1840, Bishop Bourget asked the widow Rosalie Cadron-Jetté to take a young, unmarried pregnant woman into her home. This request was followed by others until finally he asked her to leave her own home and children, rent a house, and manage it as a home for unwed mothers. This was the beginning of the Refuge Ste-Pélagie in 1845. Three years later, Rosalie Cadron-Jetté and seven other women founded the Congregation of the Soeurs de Miséricorde to care for women who "needed to hide."[3] The babies were then looked after by the Grey Nuns. This arrangement lasted until 1889, when the Soeurs de Miséricorde established their own crèches. By 1920 the hospital had a school of nursing and was used by students at the University of Montreal medical school for their obstetrical training.[4]

It is difficult to establish whether or not the rise in the number of "illegitimate" births reflects the economic difficulties of the twenties and thirties. Admissions remained stable, limited as they were by the number of available beds. Yet we know that the total number of births by single women in Quebec rose from 2.9 per cent of live births in 1931 to 3.4 per cent in 1939.[5] In 1933, the Miséricorde Hospital in Montreal and the one in Quebec City were full and were turning women away. In Montreal, the Hôpital de la Miséricorde began to restrict admission to women who were residents of the city and in their seventh month or later. We ought not to conclude too hastily, however, that illicit sex was on the rise. The illegitimacy rate rose only from 3 per cent in 1930 to 3.2 per cent in 1933; the pressure on the two Miséricorde hospitals came about because private maternity hospitals were closing as a result of the depression.[6]

The archives, registers, and medical files of the Hôpital de la Miséricorde in Montreal permit us to construct a profile of the woman who came to the Dorchester Street institution. As we might expect, she was usually French-Canadian and Catholic; only occasionally was an Irish, Italian, or Lithuanian woman admitted, but Anglophone women were usually directed to other agencies, like the Salvation Army. Even if she came from outside Montreal, a close female relative – a mother, an aunt, or a cousin – was likely to accompany her on admission. But the mother was the least likely to be present, not merely because she was being kept in ignorance of her daughter's condition but because 27.7 per cent of single mothers had lost their own mothers (and 25.8 per cent their fathers).[7] She was usually a young domestic servant. Sixty per cent of the women were between eighteen and twenty-two years old, 47 per cent of them were domestic servants, and 31 per cent lived with their families. Only 5.7 per cent worked in factories or offices. Now and then a schoolgirl, a nurse, or a teacher sought admission.[8]

The occupations recorded in the register may give us a false impression of the number of domestic servants. The women may have come to Montreal to disguise their condition once they had become pregnant and then taken a job in a private household while waiting to be admitted to Miséricorde. Similarly, it is difficult to determine their true place of residence. Of the women who gave a Montreal address, some had been there only a very short time.

The occupation and address of the patients allow us partly to infer their social origins; their fathers' occupations allow us a slightly greater precision. As an institution supported by the state, where the inmates were able to work off the cost of their confinement, the hospital accepted a very large number of women who could not have afforded private care. Among them there were some daughters of lower-middle-class fathers or tradesmen, but the fathers of most were farmers and labourers, when they were not actually unemployed. All in all, patients at the Miséricorde represented the broad lower levels of Quebec society; the narrow upper ranges were altogether absent.

Coming as they did from deprived circumstances, the women presented the kind of medical problems associated with poor nutrition and inadequate living conditions. They received a medical examination upon admission and had access to care in case of complications. The medical records do not tell us very much about their state of health. This was not the first pregnancy for 16 per cent of the women. As an indication of their general health, their recorded weight is meaningless, as it represents their weight when pregnant and their usual weight is not indicated.[9] A large number had bad teeth that had to be extracted in the hospital. Venereal disease was common. In 1928 the provincial health service treated more than half, or 344 patients, for VD at the

Miséricorde.[10] According to the medical records, 38 per cent suffered from gonorrhea and 3.7 per cent had positive Wasserman tests for syphilis. There was, however, an improvement in the syphilis rate, which exceeded 8 per cent of admissions in 1930 but never went above 6 per cent after 1936.[11] It is difficult to measure the effect of the anti-venereal campaign on the infection rate since the Bennett government cut federal funding for the campaign in 1931 as an austerity measure. More refined studies are needed to connect education and screening campaigns with the decreasing rate of syphilitic infection in a particular group. More fortunate than most of the women of their social background, the Miséricorde patients obtained diagnosis and treatment that they might otherwise have been denied. Their stay in the hospital was not necessarily more attractive on this account, however.

Although the women had certainly not become pregnant single-handedly, they were extremely reluctant to furnish any information, however vague, about the fathers of their children. The fathers' listed occupations lend little support for the staple of romance fiction – the seduction and betrayal of the young domestic worker. If the woman sometimes suggested that the father was a manager or a student, it may be assumed that her employer or his son was to blame. But most of the time, the partner belonged to the same social class as the woman herself – he was a chauffeur, a delivery man, a farm worker. The hospital wanted to know if the father drank or smoked, but the significance of positive responses is unclear. After December, 1937, information regarding the nationality and height of the father was demanded, but the data are irregular and imprecise. The image of the father, whom the nuns liked to call the accomplice,[12] is shrouded in a vagueness that arises out of indifference, unfamiliarity, or simply a desire to protect one's privacy.

During her isolation at Miséricorde, which could last for months or even a year, the boarder was provided with a new identity. On registration, she received an "imposed name" drawn from an existing stock of names bestowed on generations of single mothers since the nineteenth century. These names were not in common use but were highly unusual, like Héraïs, Calithène, Potamie, Rogata, Macédonie, Gemelle, Nymphodore, Extasie, and Symphorose. If these names were not peculiar enough, others were fraught with meaning, like Humiliane and Fructeuse.[13] The names were assigned in alphabetical order and when, after many months, the list was exhausted, it started all over again from the beginning. Along with her new identity, which assured her anonymity among her fellow inmates, the boarder acquired a uniform. The two dollars it cost represented the first of her debts. In exceptional cases, some paying boarders occupying private rooms would wear a veil for the entire length of their stay to assure absolute secrecy.

From the moment she registered until the day she left, the unwed mother, or penitent (*repentante*) as the nuns called her, would be cut off from the world and could count on the vigilance of the sisters to protect her secret.

Except during Lent and Advent, she could receive visitors in the parlour once a week, but visitors were confined to close relatives who were provided with a card with the boarder's "imposed name" on it. No card, no visit, as the mother of a young woman from out of town learned to her sorrow. Having left her card at home, she could hardly afford the fare for a return visit. Discretion was assured even in the case of a mother inquiring whether her thirty-four-year-old daughter was a patient. The director, Sister Tharcisius, answered, "If your daughter was always a good girl, what are you worried about?" [14]

This anonymity was extended to the child from the moment of birth. The mother evidently had little say in the name given her child. All the babies born in a month bore the same surname; it might be that of a nurse or intern on duty. First names were assigned in alphabetical order. To a mother who wanted a note so that she could visit her child in the crèche at Trois-Rivières and who asked about the names of the child's godparents, Sister Tharcisius wrote that the names were not necessary and, in any event, the godparents were absolute strangers, being "a nurse and one of our interns." [15] Assigned godparents and names chosen at random both contributed to a depersonalization of the connection between mother and child. Frequently, baptismal certificates indicate the child was born of "no known parentage," as if the existence of the mother herself was a mystery. [16]

The Miséricorde was a peculiar institution in that boarders usually entered voluntarily, if we leave social pressures aside for the moment, but were subjected to strict isolation and strong discipline once inside. A brief one-page prospectus described the terms of admission, the cost for single or double rooms or wards ($90, $60, and $8 a month), and a fee of $155, $130, or $120 for the cost of the delivery and adoption fees. The new boarder was told that she would have to give six months of service to the hospital starting two weeks after the birth of her child in order to repay the cost of her care and the adoption fees. Any time spent working at the hospital before delivery could be credited against the six months. Death of the child either at birth or afterwards did not change the terms; in fact, a burial charge of $25 was added to the bill. [17] Even though these terms were laid out in the prospectus, the length of time to be served surprised many women, especially when the baby died.

Although 53 per cent of the inmates were over twenty-one, all were considered minors regardless of their age. Visits were controlled and correspondence censored. Letters could only be written on Sundays, and not at all during Lent and Advent. If a patient tried to escape, she was promptly retrieved by a detective. The pregnant single woman was viewed not only as equivalent to a child but also as a criminal. If the father was termed an "accomplice," then the mother was his partner in crime.

As a matter of fact, although these women were seen as criminals, many of them were themselves victims of crime. About 3 per cent of the women were under the age of sixteen. If they were of "previously chaste character," according to section 210 of the Criminal Code, the father of the child would be guilty of seduction and subject to five years in jail. If the woman was between sixteen and seventeen, as 11 per cent were, "and of previously chaste character," he was liable to two years in prison. If he was over twenty-one and she under that age, and he had promised to marry her, he was still guilty of seduction and liable to a year's sentence.[18] Very few of the seduction cases tried in court each year resulted in conviction.[19] To seduce a feeble-minded woman or an employee was also a criminal act, but it is impossible to estimate the number of single women who were victims of these crimes or of incest.

Whatever the circumstances surrounding the single mother's pregnancy, great care was taken to shield the world at large from her presence. Once inside the institution, it was very difficult to escape its walls. In vain did the mothers of some of the inmates implore the hospital to release their daughters before the six months were up because "people were beginning to talk" about their long absence. In another case, a mother wrote of her fear that her husband would suspect the cause of his daughter's being away so long when he returned from the logging camp and found her not at home.[20] Sister Tharcisius refused the request. The nuns argued that the younger members of the family had to be protected from the scandal their older sister had caused.[21] A father wrote that he could not telephone the hospital, nor did he want the nuns to call him about the birth of his grandchild, since people listened in on the party line he shared with twenty families. He also asked that all letters come in a plain envelope, since the post office workers would recognize the Dorchester Street address and "find out."[22] The requirement for secrecy explains why one young woman fled the hospital when she recognized a new boarder.[23]

While the world was being protected from her presence, the single mother found herself reduced to the status of a child. Depending on her behaviour, she could earn good conduct marks, which could shorten her stay by two weeks, or demerits, which had the opposite effect. Trying to smuggle out a letter, for example, resulted in a black mark.[24] One patient had to serve an extra month for striking a child and keeping a pacifier for her own baby.[25] Two parents who arrived to pick up their daughter discovered that she had to serve an additional fortnight.[26] On

PROSPECTUS

Hopital Catholique de la Maternité

de Montréal

Sous la direction

des Soeurs de Miséricorde

Fondée en 1845.

⇔⊃⇒

Le but de cette Institution est de fournir un asile aux femmes qui sont sur le point de devenir mères, et de leur offrir, avec les soins corporels requis, le moyen de sauver leur honneur et celui de leur famille.

Les religieuses qui ont l'administration de cet hôpital se dévouent pour le bien moral et spirituel des hospitalisées, tandis que d'habiles gardes malades sont chargées de leur donner les soins que réclame leur position.

Dans l'admission des patientes aucune distinction n'est faite à cause de la religion, de la nationalité ou de la résidence de celles qui font application, et aucune n'est refusée à cause de sa pauvreté. Seulement, celles atteintes de quelque maladie contagieuse sont exclues.

Les patientes privées sont libres d'appeler un médecin autre que celui de l'Hôpital, si elles le désirent.

Les patientes doivent fournir leur propre linge et tous leurs objets de toilette.

Les conditions de l'admission sont comme suit :

SALLE COMMUNE.

Pension par mois	**$8.00**
Adoption de l'enfant et frais de maladie	**$120.00**

PENSION PRIVEE.

Chambres doubles, par mois	**$60.00**
Adoption de l'enfant et frais de maladie	**$130.00**
Chambre strictement privée, par mois	**$90.00**
Adoption de l'enfant et frais de maladie	**$155.00**

Les remèdes sont chargés au compte de la patiente.

La pension est payable chaque mois et les autres charges sont exigibles à l'entrée.

Le décès de l'enfant à la naissance ou plus tard ne modifie en rien les conditions ci-dessus mentionnées.

Porte d'entrée pour patientes, 440, rue Dorchester Est.

Pour conditions et informations, adressez.

SECRETAIRE DES PENSIONNAIRES,

440, rue Dorchester Est,

Montréal, P. Q.

Prospectus, including fees, of the Hôpital de la Miséricorde, Montreal.

the other hand, merit points were given to women for donating their blood to their own babies or for nursing several children.[27] Good behaviour resulted in being allowed to perform certain duties, like supervising a dormitory, which could also earn merit points and an earlier release.

This treatment was justified by the view taken of the single mother in Quebec society. If she was not strong-minded and wicked, she was seen as weak and ignorant or perhaps feeble-minded. Perhaps because mentally handicapped women were more subject to abuse, single mothers were often believed to be dull-witted. A doctor writing in a Quebec medical journal in 1932 stated that "natural [i.e., illegitimate] children seem particularly vulnerable to madness. . . . It is probable, in fact, that the parents of a natural child are themselves often abnormal."[28] The nuns sometimes termed the inmates "stupid" or "idiots" in their written comments. A patient who was slow in finishing her tasks, for example, might be considered stupid. Of course, we cannot rule out passive resistance on the part of women who wanted to be expelled before their time was up or, if they had been brought in against their will by their parents, before the birth of the child. In any event, the letters intercepted by the nuns and preserved in the files seem coherent and not lacking in intelligence.

Regardless of their intelligence, a good number of the women found themselves in the Miséricorde as a result of sexual abuse, sometimes on the part of a relative. The parish priest might write a letter of recommendation observing that the young woman came from a poor but honest family and had been taken advantage of.[29] Abused or not, they were seen as in need of repentance – they had fallen and now must atone for their sin. The inmates' mothers sometimes shared this sentiment. One wrote that she hoped her daughter's stay of one year and three months would be a good lesson for her.[30] In a few cases, the parents or the parish priest wrote to ask that a young woman be kept after her six months, until she turned twenty-one, or even longer, working in return for her room and board and being protected from the outside world and her own weakness. A parish priest wrote to Sister Tharcisius that he would be "happy for both the parents and for their daughter Y. if you could decide to keep her with you, like another of the sisters, among the penitent girls. I am convinced that only thus will she be protected from further misfortunes which await her at home."[31] These cases were referred to the Soeurs du Bon-Pasteur d'Angers, who had a home for young delinquent women. Many were most reluctant to go, for transferring to the reform school meant entering an even more restrictive atmosphere.[32]

The women at the Miséricorde were confined both to avoid scandal and to encourage them to reform. The rules were intended to form good habits. They rose very early, performed domestic tasks under close supervision, and were required to attend chapel three times a day. They were enveloped in an atmosphere of humility, repentance, and atonement. As Sister Tharcisius wrote to a woman who was coming back for a second stay, "Poor lamb, wounded by the thorns along the path, no one will reproach you if you are repentant, submissive, and humble."[33]

The work performed by the women at the Hôpital de la Miséricorde had both a moral and an economic intention. The stated purpose of the six months of service was to pay for the costs of delivery and medical treatment and the care of the child who was to be left behind. If the baby was placed for adoption, then the term of service was reduced to three months. If the baby died, the mother was still liable for six months of work to pay for the cost of the burial. Leaving a baby at the crèche cost a dollar a day for board, while labour was rated at being worth $20 a month. Days lost to illness did not count.[34] But economic considerations alone did not dictate the length of stay – those conduct marks, good or bad, also played a part. In addition, external considerations also had an effect – in 1933 a shortage of beds meant that some residents were allowed to leave a month early.

Not surprisingly, an examination of the correspondence reveals considerable confusion about the period of service that was to be exacted. Inmates wrote notes to Sister Tharcisius asking how long they still had to serve, relatives were uncertain about the release date, and many parents begged the administration to let their daughters out early because they were needed at home to help their mothers or to nurse sick members of the family. There were several cases in which families attempted to raise the money to pay off a sister's or a daughter's debt. One woman begged the nuns to release her daughter and asked if the government could not help. "I understand," she wrote, "that it is neither your fault nor that of the government," and offered to pay $75 a month. Sister Tharcisius replied that the young woman could not leave until her account had been reduced to the last $75 and "that it should not be forgotten that this is her child, not the government's nor ours although we will keep him for six years."[35] A letter from the parish priest, if it could be obtained, provided the likeliest route to an early release. Women who had nowhere else to turn went on working at the hospital for months, even years, in return for room and board. In this way they received the spiritual and material benefits of life in a religious community without being bound by vows.

Although there were women who took refuge in an institution that offered them shelter and spiritual comfort, others were forced to remain against their will to work off a non-existent debt. Someone who was interested in the welfare of the inmate, a priest or a nun from her home town, might send money for her keep but ask that she not be told, so that her stay could be prolonged to assure "as complete a recovery as possible."[36] It appears to have been a moral rather than a physical recovery that was at issue here. When the father of a patient was successful in suing the father of the baby, the hospital got $300, but the family was not reimbursed for the work the woman had done: $126.50 for her board before delivery; $50 for abandoning the child; $44 for doctor's fees and treatment.[37]

Whether its purpose was to atone for sin or to pay off a debt, the service required consisted largely of general housework, like washing furniture, or work in the scullery, in the laundry, where washing diapers was the hardest task, or in the nursery or crèche, feeding, supervising, or changing the babies and children. One mother breast-fed three or four children until, exhausted, she developed anemia and then was discharged because she was incapable of continuing to work. A few days before giving birth, wrote one boarder, "I spent the entire day ironing."[38] In 1938, a twenty-year-old English-speaking Lithuanian woman was allowed to leave after four months as a wet-nurse. She wrote to Sister Tharcisius, "My mother thinks I only do six babies, she doesn't know I have been doing thirteen of them for three months, washing them, feeding them and cleaning them."[39] One wonders how many of these thirteen she actually nursed. In another case, a doctor intervened to ask that a woman who had developed a skin rash washing furniture be permitted to stop work for forty days. She was then given damp clothes to fold and told by the doctor to stop if she felt weak and to take a tonic three times a day.[40] It is difficult to argue that this sort of work was intended solely for moral reform, since the private patients were exempt from all work before their delivery, except for "fancy needlework for their own use, and reading," and did not, of course, work afterward because they had paid the fees.[41] On the other hand, a Protestant was sent on her way after three months of service because, "as a Protestant, she will not be able to derive any spiritual benefit."[42]

Faced with the prospect of having to work for many months after the birth that would relieve her of the evidence of her sin, many an inmate rebelled and sought to shorten her term of service. Comments by the nuns in the files give glimpses of cases of passive resistance, if not tacit sabotage. The severe limitations on contact with the outside world stimulated more revolt. Desperate women threw letters out of the windows or tried to sneak them out with visitors or fellow inmates leaving the institution. We only know about those who got caught and whose letters were intercepted.[43]

Supervisors reported the breaches of the rules they observed, but how many did they miss? The best way to get expelled quickly was to be insubordinate, to use vulgar language, or to talk about shocking subjects, yet only 4 per cent were discharged for these reasons.[44] A tiny minority managed to escape without being returned. A detective brought in by the authorities usually managed to retrieve those who tried to get away. When a rebellious boarder threatened to escape in August, 1938, a detective accompanied her as she was being transferred to another institution run by the same order in Sault-aux-Récollets in suburban Montreal.[45] In the case of minors the nuns were acting *in loco parentis,* but in the case of adults they were abusing their authority, as a lawyer for one of the inmates successfully argued in securing her release.[46] But very few had the education, the contacts, or the financial resources to seek judicial relief. Closely guarded, often unfamiliar with the city, lacking sympathetic relatives to turn to, and threatened with a police pursuit and a longer sentence if they tried to escape, even rebellious women were reluctant to act.

Open revolt, in the form of an escape attempt that involved considerable risk, was the most overt manifestation of rebellion. For most boarders, even passive resistance was out of the question. Women who were depressed, frequently abandoned by their lovers, cast out from the family setting, and working hard all day despite the discomforts of pregnancy had little energy left for defiance. Like their mothers, most of them would have internalized the traditional patriarchal religious values that justified their punishment. They and their sexual partners had violated society's rules and they and, in time, their children would have to pay.

Confronted with an unwanted pregnancy, many of the women had attempted some kind of abortive procedure, from taking hot mustard baths to inserting an implement into the cervix. Not everyone admitted it, but this information appears on 5.1 per cent of their medical records.[47] Short of abortion, the surest way of evading the social consequences of an out-of-wedlock pregnancy was to marry the father. Canada and Quebec do not keep statistics on births occurring within six months of marriage and, except by consulting parish records, we cannot estimate the incidence of premarital pregnancies. The letters retained by the hospital indicate that a certain number of men claimed they intended to marry the mother when their financial situation improved, after they found a job, for example. Some, in fact, did keep their word and the child was recovered by its natural parents. Some parents prohibited their daughter from keeping in touch with her lover, and their correspondence ended up in her file, without ever reaching its destination, even though she was no longer a minor.[48] The nuns observed on at least one occasion that the mother had married a drunk whom she did not love in order to give her baby a name.[49] A few times a year marriages took place in the hospital chapel either before the baby's birth or, more often, when the woman was about to leave with her child. If the father was acceptable, both the parents and the nuns considered marriage the best solution, as it permitted the woman to be reintegrated into society in the approved role of married mother.[50] As Sister Tharcisius explained to the mother of a boarder, "The best advice is to let her get married if the young man is agreeable. . . . It's the best solution because she is not drawn to the religious life and work is hard to find."[51] The ideal solution often remained entering a convent.

The complete rehabilitation of the penitent sometimes required a permanent rejection of the world and its temptations. The most pious could enter the Madelon, named for Saint Mary Magdalene, and become Oblates. According to Sister Tharcisius, the conditions of admission were good health and good will. After spending a few months as a Daughter of Saint Marguerite, patron saint of new mothers, the candidate was issued a habit and a new name; she then entered the order on July 22, the feast day of Saint Mary Magdalene. The Oblates did not observe the strict discipline of other religious orders. They were not required to fast, but they could receive visitors only once a month and were not allowed to go out at will. They worked for the nuns, the stronger ones in the kitchen, the others doing sewing or housework.[52] In this way they could atone for their sins for the rest of their lives. At least one mother wrote her daughter recommending she expiate her fault by renouncing her life and entering this subordinate order, which would be happy to welcome her.[53]

A very small number entered the Madelon. Those who did not have a religious vocation had to deal with their immediate responsibility for the children they had borne and who were neither wanted nor "legitimate." Single mothers were generally encouraged to keep their children. As early as 1915, the Women's Directory of Montreal, which was involved in reforms for single mothers, sought to keep mother and child together to encourage breast-feeding, which had the further advantage of reducing infant mortality.[54] In 1931, the feminist Idola Saint-Jean recommended to the Royal Commission on Social Services (Monpetit Commission) that the single mother keep her child as a "safeguard" for her. She argued that not only the mother but the child would benefit from the warmth and maternal care that no institution could provide.[55] While experts encouraged single mothers to keep their children either for their own or the child's benefit, only one in eight of the patients actually left the Miséricorde with the baby. The "illegitimate" child was the legal responsibility of the mother; it was a crime to neglect or abandon it. She was required to take care of it, though the law allowed for easy adoption.[56] Many nevertheless refused to sign the papers that would permit their children to be put up for adoption. They hoped to marry or even to save enough so that one day they could retrieve their babies. This hope proved an idle dream for most, who sooner or later resigned themselves to signing the necessary documents.

For over a third of the mothers, however, long-term care for their babies did not become an issue, since the children did not survive their first year. At the beginning of the 1930s, Montreal had the unfortunate reputation of having one of the highest infant mortality rates in Canada, if not in the Western world: it fell from 125 per 1,000 in 1931 to 72 per 1,000 in 1938.[57] At the Miséricorde, 37.7 per cent of the infants born between 1929 and 1939 died in their first year, primarily of preventable diseases such as gastro-enteritis or pulmonary complaints.[58] In the hospital, the deaths of infants under one year of age underwent a marked decline in the decade, falling from 43 per cent in 1930 to 27 per cent in 1939, which mirrors the trend in Quebec and in Canada. Since the physical conditions inside the institution changed hardly at all in the period, the decrease can only be attributed to the causes commonly identified by physicians and social historians – better nutrition and an improvement in standards of sanitation.[59]

For the sisters, and even for some mothers, the death of a child was almost an occasion to rejoice. To a mother who wrote that she could not forget her child and wanted to know his whole name, Sister Tharcisius wrote, "Our Mother in Heaven has herself taken care of little Adrien. She came and got him last May. He is now a little angel up there in heaven, watching over his *maman*."[60] This was written in November, six months after Adrien's death. In the same spirit, the director wrote to a grandfather, "Dear Sir: We regret to say that the baby born to E.C. is dead. Thank God for this great favour."[61] Conscious of the weight of a life of poverty and shame, the mothers wanted their children to be spared such an end. A nineteen-year-old, who had left the hospital just two weeks after giving birth, provides an eloquent expression of this sentiment in a letter she wrote to Sister Tharcisius: "If the Good Lord would come to take her away and make her a little angel in heaven, I would be happy because who can say that she will not be miserable later on I know that she will maybe curse me some day, but I have to accept my fate, because I wanted to do what I did." She did not need to fear her daughter's curse, since the baby died when it was nineteen days old.[62]

Even if it was less painful for some mothers to forget their infants and wish them an easy death or a generous adoptive family, others continued to write the nuns, even after they had signed the adoption papers, for news about the weight, behaviour, and health of their babies. The information provided was not always accurate, perhaps to allay fears, perhaps because it referred to the wrong child. One mother wrote to ask if her child was dead so she could stop worrying about her. In April, she was informed that "she was well and always amiable"; shortly thereafter, she was informed that the child had died the previous December.[63]

While Sister Tharcisius herself encouraged women to keep their children, most could not and, after leaving the hospital, a large number took up positions as domestic servants. The "luckiest" were picked by a doctor to serve his family.[64] Most of them tried to start a new life far from their home town, hoping that their past would remain buried.

But if the woman were to take up her life as if nothing had happened, she could not keep her child, whereas the law, the child-care specialists, and the Church itself made the mother primarily responsible for its welfare. Thus she was caught in a contradiction that could only generate profound feelings of guilt and incompetence. As an example, there are the parents who, seventeen years later, wrote to ask about their child and acknowledged that "The older we get, the more we think about him – it doesn't go away."[65]

To survive economically and socially, the single mother rarely had the choice of whether or not to abandon her child. Jobs were hard to find during the Great Depression and domestic service remained the principal employment for single women in Quebec. Few would employ a single woman with a child. In 1937 the city of Montreal, on orders from the provincial government, cut single mothers from the welfare rolls.[66] Economic conditions forced many women to place their children in institutions and offer them for adoption. They were perhaps unaware that the number of adoptions was falling during the depression and that children placed with the nuns were very likely to remain in their care until adolescence. The social stigma of illegitimacy would pursue the child for its entire life. The label appeared in the parish registers and some religious orders did not accept bastard children, cutting them off from the highest aspiration of the believing Catholic. A mother could well feel guilty for condemning her child to a life of discrimination by putting her own welfare first. In this context, the expressions of relief at the death of a child are not surprising. As one grandmother wrote to Sister Tharcisius, "We are satisfied. The baby is dead, the past erased."[67]

Hidden, punished, perhaps rehabilitated, the women who sought refuge at the Hôpital de la Miséricorde were taking advantage of a service that prevailing social attitudes had made invaluable. Whatever the intentions of the nuns may have been, how did the hospital inmates view the period they spent washing diapers, peeling potatoes, and scrubbing floors? The letters that were intercepted and kept in the files may not tell the whole story of how the boarders lived, since they were written by the dissatisfied. Some letters, written by the genuinely repentant, expressed gratitude to Sister Tharcisius. Others, more common, talk of tears, exhaustion, depression, and even thoughts of

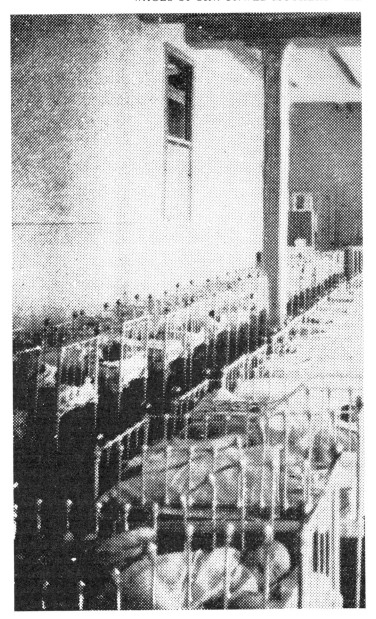

The Hôpital de la Miséricorde. *Maclean's,* December 6, 1958.

suicide. Unhappiness was to be expected and the authorities viewed it as a sign of repentance. Sister Tharcisius wrote to a former patient with whom she had kept up a warm correspondence and who planned to come to Montreal for a visit, "You will certainly be happy to see once again the chapel where you prayed so often and shed so many tears."[68]

Except for the wholly destitute who had nowhere to turn and for whom the hospital represented a refuge from a cruel world, we may assume that the majority of young women within its walls hoped to leave as soon as possible. Since they had accepted the conditions on admission, they had little choice but to resign themselves, perhaps trying to earn good marks to speed their release or begging their parents or boyfriend to find the money to pay off their debt. But the nuns, of course, had no intention of merely providing a pleasant haven safe from prying eyes.

As a refuge, the hospital guaranteed concealment. The protection it offered extended beyond the women who sought asylum there to their families and to the larger society that was shielded from the scandal that the presence of a pregnant single mother generated. Once she had lost her virginity, whether willingly or not, a woman became, according to the popular expression, "debauched." Few young men could be expected to choose such a woman as a wife and mother of his children. Concealing both the pregnancy and the child was the only way in which she might hope to resume a "normal" life, to marry and to become a mother once again, but this time in the only approved fashion. In addition, the austerities of the spiritual regime reflected the hopes of the nuns for a genuine reformation.

The means adopted to assure anonymity and to produce rehabilitation indicate the degree of social intolerance of a kind of behaviour that was hardly uncommon but that remained insupportable. Society dealt severely with those who had failed to observe the approved sexual codes. These single women may have accomplished their maternal destiny, but by doing so outside of marriage they were seen to have perverted the ideal of motherhood. In a society where the patriarchal family was absolutely fundamental, this perversion of the "natural" female function appeared as a potent assault on the very foundations of society itself.

7

Commercial Sex: Prostitution

Motherhood, as we have seen, was the primary justification for female sexuality. The satisfaction of the physical needs of the husband occupied a distant second place. If sexuality was not accompanied by maternity or if it took place outside the bonds of matrimony, then it was evil, whatever form it might take: masturbation, lesbianism, extramarital heterosexual liaisons, contraception. From the official point of view, those women who offered their sexual services to various and impersonal partners in order to earn a living represented a perversion of sexuality. Commercial sex met a demonstrated need and, for those who cared to look, could be found, one way or another, in every town of any size at all. The clientele in Quebec City was drawn largely from the port and from the university; Hull and Trois-Rivières were regularly visited by men coming down from the logging camps.[1] Prostitution was not altogether unknown in the smaller centres, either. In Joliette, for example, in 1925, the chief of police received a number of complaints about three "girls of ill repute," whom he arrested and threw out of town.[2] Montreal was certainly headquarters of prostitution, however. The women working in the trade constituted a group that placed itself beyond social expectations and the law.

Prostitution might exist publicly, in known brothels, or less openly in the bars and streets, in open or closed houses, and in cheap hotels. It was estimated that three-quarters of all illicit sexual transactions took place in the red-light district, a well-known area of Montreal used for this purpose since the nineteenth century. Less easy to perceive was more casual prostitution, associated with the bars, streets, and dance halls and widespread in the area west of Bleury, in the St. George district. The rooming-houses and one-night cheap hotels on University, Peel, and Stanley were not often troubled by the forces of law and

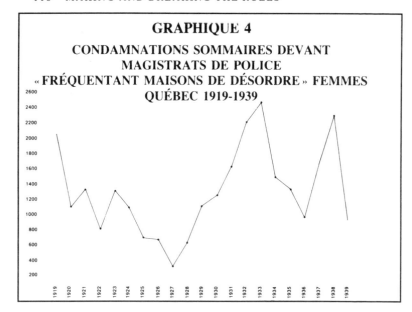

GRAPHIQUE 4

CONDAMNATIONS SOMMAIRES DEVANT MAGISTRATS DE POLICE « FRÉQUENTANT MAISONS DE DÉSORDRE » FEMMES QUÉBEC 1919-1939

Figure 4. Summary Convictions in Police Court of Women "Found-ins," Quebec, 1919-1939

SOURCE: Canada, *Annual Reports on crime statistics*, 1919-1939.

order, even when the prostitutes were clearly working the Café Baghdad on Notre Dame, the massage parlours, or the area around Windsor Station.[3]

Depending on what particular axe the commentator had to grind, the estimates of the number of women engaged in the trade vary widely. The police remarked that the 100 houses they were aware of in 1918 had been reduced to seventy-five or eighty by 1923. Judge Amédée Geoffrion, the Montreal recorder, placed their number between ninety and 100, while the social reformers who were working in the area put the total at 200 or even 300. Each house might employ six to ten women, while the larger ones, like the brothel at 92 Cadieux Street, run by Lillian Russell, alias Madame Balthazar Scheller, might house thirty to fifty.[4] The women who worked the streets and bars, some of them on a part-time basis, could be found over a wider area and were even less likely to be brought to book than the women who worked in the more established houses. There were probably as many of them, however, their numbers fluctuating with unemployment rates and economic problems. The women in the organized traffic, whose activities were easily identified, were the object of a lengthy debate concerning their legitimacy and the degree of acceptance that should be extended to them, and therefore there is a considerable body of information about them. The others appear largely in the vagrancy statistics.

Brothel inmates, being well documented, lend themselves readily to a study of prostitutes and their working conditions. Through the writings of social reformers anxious to rid the big cities of vice, the testimony of witnesses appearing before the police commission inquiry in 1924, the archives of Recorder's Court and Montreal Sessions Court, where we can find the evidence presented at the trials of important pimps, and the crime columns of the daily papers, we can get a view of a world ordinarily unwilling to reveal itself. It was indeed an underworld, one that protected itself discreetly, a world at once wide open and firmly closed.

According to the Montreal police chief, the teenagers who ended up in houses of prostitution had usually come to town from the country to work as domestics; they would be approached on a night out by acquaintances or procurers who offered them a way to make a tempting amount of money. "We know only too well," wrote Julien Saint-Michel in *Le Monde ouvrier,* "what the city does to rosy and buxom Quebec lasses who come here to earn their living and find something altogether different."[5] Those who were already in the city might want to leave hard, ill-paid work, in a laundry, for example. Most of them were probably unemployed, unskilled, uneducated, in a strange city far from home, and likely to appreciate the room, the meals, and the money a brothel offered.

Reformers, like Dr. Alfred K. Haywood of the Montreal General Hospital and Owen Dawson, treasurer of the boy's reform school at Shawbridge, commented on the presence of active recruiters in the train stations and hotels to tempt young country girls into the houses of prostitution. Father Gauthier of St. Jacques parish in the heart of the red-light district remarked on the activity of recruiters outside Montreal who promised big money in the city to young women who were working for a pittance. Some of them would be "lost" in their boarding house; others swore to their doctors that they had been drugged beforehand.[6]

In this discussion we hear the echoes of the white slave trade, which was believed to involve young women against their will and to which American and British authors attributed around 10 per cent of all prostitution.[7] This traffic, which occasioned considerable alarm before the war, became less and less a matter of concern during the twenties, though it was still discussed. In 1922, a sensational series of articles in the daily *La Patrie* alerted its readers to "base individuals" who "put on dances, offer young girls a chance in the movies, and sprinkle mysterious perfumes." Many parents had already complained that their

MONTREAL, SAMEDI, 22 FEVRIER 1919

UNE PLAIE QUI A ENVAHI LES QUARTIERS FASHIONABLES

Ce que contient le deuxiè- me rapport du Comité des Seize. La tolérance produit des effets désastreux.

La traite des blanches

Le deuxième rapport du Comité des Seize vient d'être publié. Il traite des moyens propres à supprimer le vice commercialisé et à prévenir ses conséquences terribles. On se souvient que le premier rapport traitant principalement des conditions du vice à Montréal, de sorte que les deux rapports se complètent l'un l'autre: l'un indique le mal et l'autre le remède.

Le vice commercialisé s'est répandu si rapidement dans notre ville qu'il a envahi les quartiers les plus fashionables. Il est devenu si flagrant et si pratique avec un tel sans gêne que les citoyens jusqu'ici les plus sceptiques commencent à s'émouvoir et jettent un cri d'alarme qui, espérons-ie, sera entendu pour l'avenir de nos

qui comme l'immoralité de deux êtres consentantes et qui néglige de considérer la prostitution comme apportant la ruine physique et morale aux uns et des projets illicites aux autres."

A MONTREAL

"Quand bien même on en finirait bientôt avec le système de tolérance à Montréal, les effets désastreux de la période pendant laquelle ce système a été en vigueur, se feront sentir longtemps. A cause de ce système de tolérance, nous rencontrons des difficultés presque insurmontables pour combattre le vice commercialisé ici. En premier lieu nous avons un nombre considérable de maisons malfamées, desquelles plusieurs sont reconnues comme tolérées depuis nombre d'années. Nous avons une population qui est prête à croire soit qu'il est nécessaire d'enrayer le vice commercialisé, soit qu'il est impossible de ce faire."

LES VICTIMES

"Nous savons que les victimes elles-mêmes ont une opinion profondément erronée sur ce sujet et que la grande majorité des citoyens de Montréal ne veulent pas combattre assez longtemps pour changer la situation. Nous avons un département de police qui est exposé aux dangers inévitables de la corruption

poursuivre leurs exploiteurs", dit le rapport.

Comme mesures répressives, on mentionne entr'autres les suivantes: L'abolition des districts "red light";

La fermeture des maisons malfamées;

Poursuivre les tenanciers et les propriétaires, etc., etc.

Enfin, il y a bien d'autres faits intéressants dans le rapport du Comité des Seize et nous croyons que nos lecteurs devraient s'en procurer une copie.

Voici les noms des officiers et des membres du Comité des Seize:

OFFICIERS.

Président: Rév. Herbert Symonds;
Vice-président: Owing P. Rexford;
Hon. trésorier: Alex. Falconer;
Hon. secrétaire: Mlle K. Moore;
Secrétaire: Mlle Lucy C. Phinny;
Secrétaire: Owen Dawson

MEMBRES.

M. l'abbé Henri Gauthier, N. J. Dupuis, Mlle L. E. F. Barry, Mlle Margaret Campbell, MM. John Bradford, James Carruthers, W. B. Colley, Zéphirin Hébert, J. Auguste Richard, F. W. Stewart, le Dr W.

"A Plague Invading Fashionable Districts": report on the extent of the white slave trade, which, according to reformers, menaced all social classes. *La Patrie,* 22 février 1919.

daughters had disappeared.[8] In Hull, the chief of police in 1923 reported on an important white slave traffic linked to the consumption of alcohol.[9]

The traffic in innocent victims, long a staple of popular fiction, could not fail to arouse the feelings of right-thinking people. The extent of the problem, which was probably exaggerated, defies every attempt to quantify it. One trial for white slavery in 1932 gives some idea of how a young girl might become involved in prostitution. Anna L., sixteen years old, left her farm family to look for work in Montreal. Soon afterwards she accepted the promise of Alfred Ménard, who owned brothels in St. Jean, of forty to forty-five dollars a week. Ménard also got Adrienne H. and Prisca D. to run away from the same village. They wanted to work as domestics and said they did not know where he was taking them. In the absence of proof, the judge could only drop the charges. The young women, after all, were a party to what had happened, were they not?[10] Without drugs, mysterious perfumes, or clear physical brutality, how could coercion be demonstrated?

For the police to win a case, they had to depend on something beyond the testimony of the women involved. In 1936, Max Kaufman was sentenced to eighteen months for having "induced and solicited women into having carnal commerce with other persons." He was incriminated after a police agent offered to sell him "a young virgin," with whom he reserved, as was his habit, the right to "first night privileges."[11] He was a repeat offender known to the police, which aided in his conviction.

Physical constraint was a relative matter for many young women – economic necessity was pressing and the attraction of making an income several times larger than they could expect from domestic service or waiting on tables tempted many of the more naive. They did not think long and hard before entering the trade but often hoped only to land themselves in a temporary and lucrative line of work.

Single mothers with nowhere to go and, according to Dr. Haywood, even young girls who had stayed out all night and were afraid to go home sometimes took shelter in one of these shady houses. Having no money at all, teenagers would embark on a predictable path. Antoinette H. was in the reform school run by the Soeurs du Bon-Pasteur from the ages of thirteen to seventeen. After she struck a nun, she was transferred to the women's prison on Fullum Street. When she got out, she went to work for Eva Pilon (Mamie Brown).[12] Indeed, without being forced into it, young women growing up in the districts where prostitution flourished might very well follow in the footsteps of their mothers and neighbours and enter an occupation that had been familiar to them from birth. Observers report that the prostitutes in the brothels or walking the streets were often thirteen or fourteen years old.[13] Doctors also remarked on the part the depression played in the upsurge of teenage vagrancy and prostitution.[14]

The young women who took up life in a brothel were entering a universe with a clear hierarchy. The building itself belonged to a man or a woman who usually lived in some other area of the city. If the proprietor knew to what use the place was being put, the rent charged would be much higher than for the other dwellings in the same street, going as high as $100 a month or even $50 a week, depending on how profitable the establishment was.[15] The "inside," that is, the business, belonged to the madam, who also usually lived somewhere else. She would come for the takings in the mornings, when the police were rarely around and she stood less chance of being picked up.

In the well-run houses, the madam employed a housekeeper to manage the business. Some large houses had two of them, working twelve-hour shifts, while Lillian Russell's famous 92 Cadieux Street had three, on eight-hour shifts.[16] The manager, identified by her big bunch of keys and her punch to keep a record of services rendered, watched over the prostitutes, maintained order in the disorderly house, and was arrested when the police made their periodic raids. It was she who was often charged with maintaining a bawdy house. The descriptions appearing in the arrest warrants are often vague and make it difficult to distinguish madams from managers and arrive at a general portrait of either one. Lillian Hoover, a well-known madam, is described as having "greying hair, tall and stout, between forty and forty-five years of age." Fleurette Gauthier is "blonde, stout, about five feet tall, and around thirty or thirty-five."[17] Out of a sample of thirty-two women who appeared in court in February and March of 1930 accused of running bawdy houses, seven were between twenty-five and thirty years old, ten between forty and fifty, but most were between thirty and thirty-five. Only two signed their names, the others making a cross. Five of their surnames sound English, but that is not a reliable guide to their ethnic origin. The majority were released on bail. Of those who were convicted, two did time, the others paid fines.[18] Some of these were retired prostitutes, but the younger ones were probably still working. If they were liable to be arrested frequently, their profits justified the risk – the madam kept half of what the prostitutes earned and paid her manager according to the profits.[19]

Madams and managers often lived with their pimps, whom they supported and who sometimes owned the premises. This was true for Anna Herscovitch, alias Madame Anita and a madam since 1921, who lived with Tony Frank, the notorious bandit who was hanged in 1924. She became the proprietor of the houses on Cadieux Street.[20] The madams assumed all responsibility for their "girls." They paid bail for them in court instead of the pimp; they paid fines, which they charged the women's accounts; they hired and fired; they determined the prices charged to the clients. They were sometimes generous, bringing food to those who were in jail or visiting their employees in the hospital when they went in for a "miscarriage." They did not, however, fail to charge the medical fees to the woman's account.[21]

At the bottom of this pyramid were the common prostitutes. The police charge sheets only mention their names and addresses, without any descriptions. Their working conditions varied according to the quality of the house. Services might cost five dollars in the better places, going down to a dollar in the seediest joints; the manager rang a bell to measure off each ten- or fifteen-minute period.[22] If she were young and healthy, the "girl" might find herself in one of the first-class houses, for example on Cadieux Street. As time went on, she would wind up in the three-dollar (or less) houses on Charlotte or St. Justin streets (later on Berger). In the lowest dives, the prostitutes would accumulate a large number of punches on their cards. One reformer who was investigating the subject reported the example of Lucienne, sixteen, who had her card punched fifty-three times between four o'clock Saturday afternoon and two o'clock Sunday morning.[23] Regardless of the class of house, the manager was the one who kept order – regulating mealtimes, clothing, and days off and imposing any punishments. Dr. Haywood, in whom a number of the women confided, was of the opinion that they were sometimes shut up in the house for weeks at a time.[24]

Compared to the pittances paid to domestic servants, sweatshop workers, or women in any of the other jobs open to unskilled workers, the daily pay of a prostitute seemed very attractive. The expenses connected with this mode of life, however, always exceeded the income. The residents of a brothel paid between two and five dollars a day rent, to which laundry charges were added. In addition, frequent purchases from the pedlars who came door-to-door gobbled up a good part of their budget – cigarettes, perfume, clothing, silks, and fur coats were all offered by the pedlars at inflated prices. The madams took a commission on these sales, even when they were buying for themselves and charging the goods to the inmates' accounts.[25]

These expenses aside, drugs, above all else, kept the prostitutes forever in debt. Drugs were endemic to the profession and the majority of the women were addicted. Both social reformers and the police exposed the presence of cocaine and heroin in the brothels. According to Owen Dawson, between 50 and 75 per cent of all prostitutes shot up "to keep up their pep and snap."[26] Father Gauthier believed that the drugs, which were everywhere in the houses of prostitution, met a need for those "with limited human resources."[27] Dr. Haywood commented on the number of prostitutes admitted to the Montreal General for an overdose and those who were brought in suffering from withdrawal symptoms while they were in police custody and who needed a shot before they could appear in court. Some of them had a morphine habit of ten grams a day and were said to conceal their "decks" of cocaine in their high heels.[28] Some observers attributed the use of narcotics to a need for something to make it possible to carry on in the sex trade; on the other hand, addiction forced some into prostitution as a way of supporting their habit.[29] Pimps were notoriously involved in drug trafficking. Tony Frank, the gang boss, ran drugs, while Joseph Labrecque, convicted for procuring in 1932, had been found guilty of drug possession in 1926.[30]

The madams were more cautious; they generally neither used nor sold narcotics. Alice Brown, convicted in 1925 both for drugs and for keeping a bawdy house, represents an unusual case.[31] John Swail, who played piano for thirty-five years in various brothels, testified before the Coderre Commission that Anna Herscovitch, who owned 333 Cadieux, required her manager to bar drug dealers from the premises.[32] Swail was aware, however, that drug use was widespread among the inmates. Judge Geoffrion viewed the madams as representing a force for order in their disorderly houses. They were not interested in risking jail for the sake of a traffic that would yield them little compared with the returns from the brothel itself, and some of them would turn cocaine pushers in to the police.[33] Nevertheless, in the opinion of both the police and the investigators, no whorehouse was free of drugs, and once hooked, the prostitutes were involved in mounting debt that would keep them trapped in their occupation.

When she became a prostitute, a woman commonly adopted a working name. Just as in the home for unwed mothers, this name both protected her and afforded her a certain anonymity. If the inmates of the Hôpital de la Miséricorde received names with improving meanings, those in the brothels preferred to pick the names of flowers. The lists of women arrested in the red-light district contain an unusual number of Roses, Blanches, and Marguerites, not to speak of Violette Deschamps, Fleurette Després, and Muguette Desbois.[34] With names like these, adopted for the occasion, it was simple to thwart the courts, for example, by substituting someone who was uninfected for another woman suffering from a venereal disease and therefore subject to a heavier fine. As for the madams, they were known by their "noms de guerre." As Flora Harris explained, "We never give our real names. We always go by our nicknames."[35] So Anna Herscovitch became Madame Anita; Rose Tremblay became Rose Latour or Rosey Jemme; Anna Lalonde, Anna Noela; and Mamie Brown, May or Eva Pilon. Judge Geoffrion admitted that a policeman filing charges "never asked the girl's name because that would only arouse suspicion."[36] She was brought to court according to the description in the warrant, where she gave a nom de guerre. One story will illustrate the kind of game both sides liked to play. A madam and six of her "girls" were supposed to appear in court but one of them failed to show up. To find out who was who, Judge Geoffrion, who had seen all of them before, had them examined to see whether one of them was tattooed with the initials "M.L." He sent someone to look for the twenty-year-old missing woman at her house and gave her the maximum sentence of three months in jail or a $100 fine.[37] The police agreed that it was useless to try to identify prostitutes by name because "when they're called the next morning, they can never remember what name they gave."[38]

If the madams commonly had English names like Lillian Russell, Flora Harris, or Mamie Brown, the managers and the prostitutes were usually Francophone. We come across few foreign-sounding names in the judicial records. Montreal does not seem to have been affected by the traffic in young Jewish women coming from Russia to New York and South America.[39] In 1923, Judge Geoffrion remarked, "After a dozen years on the bench, I can count on the fingers of one hand the number of Jewish prostitutes appearing before me."[40] The names appearing on the lists of prostitutes arrested in the red-light district during the thirties are predominantly Francophone. Even if the names themselves are fictional, the judicial documents that have come down to us are in French.

Prostitution turned out to be an extremely dangerous occupation from a number of points of view, involving as it did the risk of venereal disease, unwanted pregnancy resulting in abortion, drugs, and violence on the part of the clients. The transmission of venereal disease was directly associated with prostitution and the woman risked becoming infected from the outset.

The evidence of the incidence of these infections is unreliable, but beginning in 1919, persons found in bawdy houses were tested and the statistics compiled from these records give us some idea of the amplitude of the problem. The annual reports by the Montreal chief of police give percentages of women infected, which range from 14 per cent in 1921 to 4 per cent in 1924 and back up to 14 per cent in 1939.[41] On the other hand, public health physicians cite a much higher rate of infection. In his testimony before the Coderre Commission, Dr. Antoine-Hector Desloges, the director of the Quebec venereal disease campaign, stated that "all the prostitutes are infected with one disease or another."[42] He did, however, admit that in the absence of figures from Montreal, he was basing his opinion on numbers furnished by the "learned societies" and other North American cities.[43] Dr. Alfred K. Haywood was of the opinion that 95 per cent of the women working in the brothels were infected, while Dr. Gustave Archambault of the Provincial Health Service conceded that while all of them were infected, not all were contagious.[44] A large number of them, however, must have been contributing to the high rate of venereal infection in Quebec. Figures provided by the Provincial Health Service presented prostitution as the source of male venereal disease in 80 per cent of reported cases; 37 per cent of those infected reported that they had caught the disease in a brothel and 43 per cent from a streetwalker.[45] Without being an actual criminal, the prostitute was "biologically guilty," as Erica-Marie Benadou wrote of prostitution in France; usually infected, highly contagious, she was in "a continual criminal condition."[46]

The spread between the police figures and those of the health professionals makes it difficult to judge the rate of infection among prostitutes. According to the doctors, the examination of those found in brothels did not reveal the true nature of the problem because women could prepare for the medical examination, which did not take place until the day after they were arrested. If they were allowed to go home, they could take certain steps to conceal their condition. They were motivated to disguise their lesions less by a desire to avoid treatment than by a fear of being fired by the madam who wished to protect her trade[47] or by the fine of $100 imposed by the court on women found to be infected.[48] The medical examination was generally a cursory one and did not usually involve a blood test or a Wasserman.[49] The public health professionals, who were in daily contact with the ravages caused by syphilis and gonorrhea, probably had a tendency to exaggerate, especially when they were motivated, as was Dr. Desloges, by moral or eugenic considerations. Dr. Desloges was particularly alarmist, suggesting that syphilis shortened one's life by a third, could be transmitted to the seventh or eighth generation, and was responsible for a quarter of all cases of insanity. He viewed the red-light district as the prime area of contamination and maintained that syphilis could be transmitted by kissing or by drinking from the same glass as someone infected, and therefore he recommended "the suppression of kissing."[50]

The prostitutes had entirely different concerns. The professionals who worked in the houses were probably less diseased than might be expected. They knew what precautions to take to minimize the risk of infection. Condoms, vaginal sponges, and douches could not guarantee immunity but they could provide a certain degree of protection for a period of time. On the other hand, those who did become infected knew to use Salvarsan. For their part, the madams were interested in running clean houses and getting rid of diseased employees. The madam at 16 St. Justin Street complained to Owen Dawson that, after having paid $500 for her best dancer, who was fifteen years old, she turned out to be so infected that she had to be got rid of.[51] When they did not turn the diseased women out, they sometimes tried to obtain certificates of good health for them. Dr. Haywood reported that a madam had appeared at the Montreal General Hospital to try to buy such certificates, but she was refused.[52] Less scrupulous doctors issued false certificates for as little as fifty cents. A woman named Gaby posted her certificate at the same time that she was being treated for syphilis.[53] The fear of being dismissed or of being fined encouraged this kind of shady behaviour.

On the other hand, the streetwalkers did not have the same access to information and the kind of contacts that would permit them to avoid or conceal a disease. Despite the disagreement of the doctors about the danger casual prostitutes represented to the public health, we may assume that if they were not more frequently infected than the women who worked in the brothels, they probably became diseased sooner. Dr. Archambault was virtually the only one to maintain that streetwalkers were no more dangerous than the women in the houses because, he believed, they had fewer clients and knew them better, though why he thought this is unclear, and he claimed they were more careful because they were obliged to stay healthy. He thought that if they were sick, they went to the dispensary for treatment right away.[54] Studies conducted in France and the United States, among other places, indicate that, on the contrary, street prostitutes had a higher rate of infection.[55]

During the depression the budget cuts made by the Bennett government affected prostitutes particularly. The federal government cut its contribution to the anti-venereal disease campaign by more than half despite the increase of patients at the dispensaries who, after January, 1932, could no longer be given free medication at the hospitals.[56] These cuts certainly severely affected the most diseased prostitutes, who had counted on this assistance. Between 1931 and 1934, the number of found-ins examined decreased, as did the number of arrests, but after a brief rise in 1935, examinations continued gradually to decrease regardless of an increase in the number of arrests. The doctors were less interested in establishing a diagnosis when they knew their patients would not follow a course of treatment.

In these circumstances, regardless of the range of opinions on the matter, it was only a matter of time until a prostitute became infected. The moralists viewed infection as only what she deserved. According to Father Victorin Germain, "The debauched man or woman would be punished in the way they had sinned."[57] Although the punishment was not necessarily fatal, Dr. Desloges was hardly exaggerating when he listed the consequences of untreated syphilis: blindness, debility, and even insanity. Recognizing the risks of their trade, the prostitutes sought treatment to the best of their ability. All the same, the reformers attributed the brief careers of prostitutes to venereal disease. As Father Gauthier put it, after five or seven years, "they have had it . . . they are in the gutter, they are in the street, and then they are in the hospital."[58] Those who were part of the scene did not share these alarmist views. John Swail commented on the life span of the women he hung out with. "Twenty years they live for and never seem to die," he told Judge Coderre, who asked him about the ages of the women in the brothels.[59] His memories are coloured by nostalgia and should be taken with a grain of salt. Nevertheless, disease did not prove fatal to a large number of prostitutes – the managers and madams had all spent many years in the business.

Even if prostitutes knew more about contraception than other women, the methods they used were not infallible and pregnancy was always a worry. Some of them were able to keep their children or place them with relatives, but this was not an option for most of these single mothers. Madams, who were better off, could pay for their board and Rose David, who kept a house on the corner of St. Lawrence and St. Viateur, was supposed to have her little girls boarding at a convent, as was Anna Herscovitch.[60]

For ordinary prostitutes, abortion offered the simplest solution to an accidental pregnancy. The twenty-three-year-old prostitute reported by Dr. Haywood to have had a number of abortions was not an unusual case.[61] Unlike young domestic servants, the prostitutes in the brothels had the advantage of working in a group and for an experienced woman and thus were better able to find the resources they needed to deal with their condition. They were not, however, altogether protected against horrible consequences, such as the fate that overtook Helen R., twenty-five years old and a client of Alphonse Noël. She consulted the herbalist in order to terminate her third "premature pregnancy," was forced to have sexual relations with him, and died five days later of a uterine hemorrhage.[62] Because of the frequency with which they had sexual intercourse, coupled with the failure rate of contraceptive devices of the period, prostitutes had recourse to abortion more often than the majority of women and thus were more likely to suffer the consequences of a botched operation.

Along with venereal disease and risky abortions, and the cocaine, heroin, and morphine endemic to the business, we have to add as well the widespread use of tobacco and alcohol to complete the list of conditions likely to shorten a prostitute's life.

If the classier whorehouses were run respectably, there were many that served as hideouts for mobsters, gangsters on the run, and men involved in every kind of illegal traffic. Violence was common and prostitutes often found themselves victims of it. The madam was likely to be robbed and the workers beaten. For three nights running, the police were called to protect Flora Harris's house, which was being held up.[63] Regular prostitutes were even more vulnerable and could not altogether avoid clients who might send them to the local hospital.[64] Streetwalkers were even more likely to be victims of violence. The murder of Prudentienne Daigneault, better known as Jeanne Labbé, who was strangled in a room in the Hôtel d'Italie on St. Lawrence, is a good illustration of the kind of danger that stalked women when they were alone with their customers.[65] This violence furnished an excuse for the pimps, who offered to protect a house or, in the case of street prostitution, a whole "stable" of women. But nothing could protect them against police brutality. When Antoinette Hamel, alias Blanche Corbeil, a manager at Flora Harris's, charged Captain Sauvé with "bad treatment of women," the charges were dropped and she had to pay court costs.[66] Given the inequality between the two sides, this kind of case was extremely unusual.

As they were familiar with the women of the red-light district, the police took advantage of certain privileges before making an arrest. When, for example, Lieutenant J.B. Bricault of the provincial police appeared at Gaby Gauthier's, he had a dance, drank a beer, picked out a woman, paid five dollars for twenty minutes to go to a room with her, then arrested the madam. It was the same story when Constable Lemieux and his companion paid a visit to Lillian Hoover's. They first chose a girl from those who were sitting around the living room in their underwear, paid two dollars, went upstairs, and then proceeded to make the arrest.[67]

Since they were well known to the police, prostitutes were often called on to "make a case," particularly to inform on illegal drinking establishments or "blind pigs." In the early twenties Eva Bernard – La Grande Eva Champagne – helped Captain Roch Sauvé with five or six cases. For informing, she was given a quarter of the fine imposed, or five dollars, as well as leniency on the part of the judge who was informed about her co-operation. It was the police-customer who established the rate when favours were exchanged.[68]

Co-operating with the authorities assured that business would run smoothly and directly influenced the life of the prostitutes. The police hung out in the brothels in the district and had to be paid protection money. If she maintained cordial relations with the police, a madam was less likely to run into trouble and would always be warned when the vice squad was about to descend. Flora Harris was arrested fifteen times; such were the consequences of running an unprotected house.[69] In 1932 Joseph Labrecque, who operated houses on Hotel de Ville, admitted to paying five constables between $5 and $50 a week.[70] The Coderre Commission tried to shed some light on the various sources of police revenue but often failed to provide incontrovertible proof, aside from the admissions of the madams, who were not viewed as trustworthy witnesses. Captain Roch Sauvé earned a salary of $2,400 a year and, responding to certain rumours, attributed his wealth to his luck at the races, where he said he made $12,000 to $20,000 a year. It was impossible to prove that he had received gifts, rings, and money from Anna Lalonde or Mamie Brown.[71] As for Superintendent Pierre Bélanger, whose $6,000 a year salary was hardly adequate to support his luxurious yacht, he claimed to be lucky at cards, not on the take from Rose David.[72] These exchanges between the police and the brothel-keepers ensured the continuation of the system. For two decades, regardless of sporadic cleanup campaigns, activity in the district might be interrupted for a few hours or a few days, but the addresses remained absolutely unchanged.

The welfare and security of the inmates depended directly on their relationship with the brothel manager and in turn on her relations and those of the madam with the police. Warned in advance of an impending police raid, the manager or the madam could decide whom they would allow to be arrested – those who worked the least or who needed to be given a lesson or who were too far in debt.[73] When they were found guilty, the $25 fines would be added to their accounts.

In street prostitution the pimp played an essential role, and his contacts with the authorities defined the working conditions of the girls on the street. He was an intermediary between the police and the prostitute, negotiating with the police what area she might work and on what streets; thus when Rose Roberts was arrested in 1933, the police told her to confine herself to Stanley, Metcalfe, and Peel streets.[74] The pimp took care of the accounts, provided bail, and did very well for himself out of the arrangement. In 1932, during one of the worst years of the Great Depression, Joseph Labrecque confided to a city policeman that if it "were not for the 'provincial' it wouldn't be too bad. I'm making a hundred dollars a week clear." Labrecque was well known to lawyers, the police, and assistant court clerks, as he found himself in court three or four times a week over a period that he vaguely described as "ten or twenty years." Finally, in 1933, a zealous new chief of police, Fernand Dufresne, put an end to his career and Labrecque was found guilty of procuring and of maintaining brothels on Hotel de Ville Street.[75]

Though some women paid off the police themselves, they could not altogether establish their independence from a pimp. In 1933, for example, Jeanne Dubois, twenty-two, who generally made around $80 a week in the area near Burnside (now de Maisonneuve) and McGill College, had to pay $10 a week to Maurice Catton and $30 to the police. Even when she decided to rent her own apartment on McGill College, she had to turn to Catton. She was a woman and the landlord insisted that a man sign the lease. She denied to the court in 1932 that she had ever given Catton money, probably in order to protect him when he was accused of living off the avails of prostitution. Catton, who was born in France, was about thirty and good-looking. He lived off women working the west end of the city, near Dorchester (now René Lévesque). According to the policeman who hung around with him before he turned him in, he used to drop his women off and pick them up in a car, took their earnings, and would get very angry at the women he called lazy for not making more than $6 or $7. One of his women was only fifteen.[76]

Even more exploited were the women who waited on tables at the restaurant owned by Angelo Mastrolorido and Annie Levitsky on Vitré Street. The were paid $3 a week and housed and fed in rooms upstairs over the restaurant. Their clientele were sailors who paid fifty cents "if it was only for a minute," and $2 for the whole night. Mastrolorido's name had been brought up before the Coderre Commission in 1923; fourteen years later, in 1937, he was charged with procuring and found not guilty.[77] Considering the numbers of prostitutes in Montreal, a large number of pimps must have been exploiting their labour with impunity during this period. These were the prostitutes who most risked being arrested, as was the case of Jeanne Dubois, who was not protected on this occasion, and who was "a known vagrant, dissolute, idle, or debauched within the meaning of the law adopted to this effect in so far as she was illegally loitering on a public street, namely Burnside."[78]

In addition to these professionals were women who engaged in prostitution on a casual basis, responding to periodic economic need. In this category might fall the twenty-seven-year-old woman whose semi-invalid husband was unable to work and who prostituted herself by the night.[79] Unemployment regularly swelled the number of women on the street.

Without having a word to say in the matter, the prostitutes were controlled both by those in the business – the managers, madams, and pimps – and by those outside it, that is, the various authorities. Since the turn of the century, these women had been at the heart of the debate over the control of prostitution. The clergy, the feminists, and some reformers hoped for nothing less than the total elimination of prostitution. But the judges in Recorder's Court were lined up behind those who wanted a strict regulation of the business, to have it confined to the brothels and to subject the women to rigorous controls, including medical examination,[80] identification cards, and police surveillance. This European-inspired idea of regulation was supported by the trade unionist Gustave Francq and the journalist Julien Saint-Michel in *Le Monde ouvrier*. Without going as far as this, segregationists, like the mayor, Médéric Martin, wanted to see the houses limited to the red-light district, where the police could keep an eye on them. Most reformers, who represented a considerable pressure group from the middle of the 1920s onward, as well as public health physicians, wanted to eliminate "commercialized vice," which they defined as transactions involving a third party. In point of fact, this proposal threatened too many interests and infringed on the habits of too many customers.

Regardless of the vague gestures in the direction of suppression represented by the Coderre Commission report in 1925, the system that prevailed combined surveillance with a toleration that was conditional on relationships between the brothels and the police.[81] It was a hybrid system, subject to corruption, and it persisted despite the about-turns of social reformers in the twenties, the enthusiasm of a new chief of police at the beginning of the thirties, and the periodic zeal of police who were being pressured to make a case or settle accounts. Those who were most directly involved, the prostitutes, had no choice but to weather the effects of alternate waves of toleration and suppression.

Ideally, both morality and the law ought to have applied equally to both the prostitute and her customer. Sexual activities that took place

GRAPHIQUE 5

CONDAMNATIONS POUR DÉLITS JUDICIABLES D'UN JURY. « LUPANARS, TENANCIÈRES ET PENSIONNAIRES ». FEMMES. QUÉBEC 1919-1939

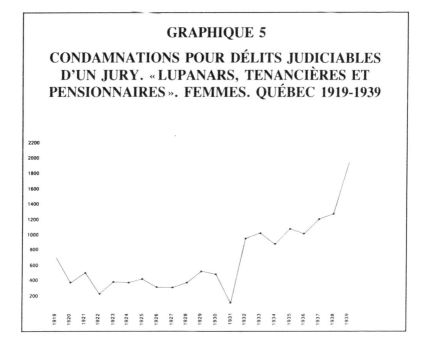

Figure 5. Convictions for Offences Subject to Jury Trial: "Brothels, Madams, and Inmates," Women, Quebec, 1919-1939
SOURCE: Canada, *Annual Reports on crime statistics*, 1919-1939.

outside the confines of marriage were sinful and persons found in a bawdy house were liable to jail sentences or fines. In practice, the double standard demanded that the parties to the offence be treated in very different ways, according to their sex. No one except the feminists took seriously the idea that they were equally guilty. We have seen the reception given to the feminists' ideas by Judge Geoffrion – five years after his interview with a representative of the MLCW who wanted the customers of the brothels to receive the same sentences as the prostitutes, he was still quoting them with derision before the Coderre Commission.[82] It was not so much the severity of the sentences demanded that outraged the judge; it was the men's vulnerability.

No social stigma attached to young men in search of an adventure or to those who had to find an outlet for their excess sexuality, or to anyone who found no contradiction in the idea of paying for sexual favours. In picking up a woman on the street, the client had little to fear. The police rarely bothered the rooming houses, where it was difficult to prove that money had been exchanged for sex. When streetwalkers found themselves before a judge, they were charged with "loitering."

The statistics on those found in bawdy houses indicate that their clientele did not enjoy immunity to arrest and a great number came before Recorder's Court. In 1934, for example, 813 women and 1,440 men appeared; in 1935, there were 1,297 women and 1,165 men.[83] The men usually got off with a $10 or $15 fine and often were spared the prescribed medical examination – in 1934, 277 men were examined; in 1935, 288. The annual report of the Montreal police indicates that in fact a tiny number of men were pronounced infected with venereal disease; in certain years, every one was declared healthy.[84] In these circumstances, it is little wonder that prostitutes continued to become infected.

As objects of public discussion and repressive policies, the prostitutes of the period are known to us only at second hand, through intermediaries. When their contemporaries leave a picture of them behind, it is modified to a greater or lesser degree by the convictions, expressed or not, of the commentator. They were not permitted a voice in the various studies made of their milieu; they speak only in gestures, which are dependent for their transmission to us on the good will of those who observed and recorded them. Their actions, however, duly noted, lead us to suspect resistance, even rebellion, within the narrow limits of their existence. The exchanging of names to confuse the forces of law and order constitutes a primary example of subversion. Once arrested, many women refused to be intimidated and avoided their court appearances. They produced all kinds of excuses or simply did not appear at all when the sitting judge had a reputation for being tough. The newspapers reported that one morning all the prostitutes called before Judge Semple, who was less understanding than Judge Geoffrion, offered an excuse: "Knowing the fraternity's habitual objections to proceedings before Recorder Semple, the court rocked with laughter as plea after plea was made for delay."[85] A study of warrants issued against forty-seven madams between February 18 and March 13, 1930, reveals that the whereabouts of fourteen of them remained "unknown."[86] Those arrested also outsmarted the doctors by taking the necessary precautions to disguise their venereal disease and thus avoided the maximum penalty the judge might impose on infected women.[87]

There was not only resistance; there was solidarity. Like the prostitutes, the madams stood in for one another to mislead the authorities. The law imposed a prison sentence on madams who were convicted on their third offence. The actual madam was therefore often absent and a manager tried to take the rap for running a bawdy house. During the extensive crackdown in 1923, the managers of different houses

Table 4
Report on the Medical Examination
of Persons Arrested in Disorderly Houses,
Montreal, 1928-1939

	Women Examined	Men Examined	Women Infected	
1928	1,433	690	58	4%
1929	2,991	1,256	582	19.5
1930*	–	–	–	–
1931	4,054	968	426	10.5
1932	3,947	969	302	7.7
1933	2,715	428	226	8.3
1934	1,944	277	306	15.8
1935	2,209	288	387	17.5
1936	2,202	293	331	15
1937	2,132	348	364	17
1938	2,023	322	293	14.5
1939	2,452	404	343	14

* Data unavailable for 1930.
SOURCE: Montreal, *Annual Reports of the police department, 1929-1939*.

swapped places night after night so that the same people would not be arrested over and over.[88]

Although prostitutes were not ordinarily considered credible witnesses, law enforcement authorities were liable to blackmail as a result of their connections to the brothels. According to Captain Sauvé, the judge of the Recorder's Court never accepted the testimony of a prostitute unless it was corroborated by a police officer.[89] Nevertheless, at the Coderre Commission, the madams who testified were taken seriously and their testimony embarrassed more than one member of the force. A certain familiarity grew up between the police and the prostitutes, which did not prevent women from thumbing their noses at the authorities and, on one occasion, from throwing a bucket of water over a constable's head.[90] This boldness can be seen both as part of the game and as an attempt to establish certain rules. Dominated by both the legal system and the madams, prostitutes had little room in which to assert themselves. They saw their work, indeed their lives, appropriated by everybody who could made a profit from them. They were public women, and to be controlled, the antithesis of public men, who personified the forces that controlled them.

Table 4 continued

Men Infected		Women Not Infected		Men Not Infected	
19	2.75%	1,372	95.7%	671	97.25%
18	1.4	2,409	80.5	1238	98.6
–	–	–	–	–	–
4	0.4	3,628	89.5	964	99.6
0	0	3,645	92.3	969	100
0	0	2,489	91.7	428	100
0	0	1,638	84.2	277	100
0	0	1,822	82.5	288	100
3	1	1,871	85	290	99
0	0	1,769	83	348	100
0	0	1,730	85.5	322	100
2	0.5	2,109	86	402	99.5

There is a strange contradiction between the toleration extended to prostitutes and their clients and the strictness with which sexual offences were treated in public discussion. On the one hand we see general threats of stern repression; on the other, the complicity of those authorities directly involved in the sex trade or their reluctance to interfere with too many vested interests. Prostitution occupied a place in the universe that was the polar opposite of middle-class Catholic belief; it was permitted, but it was subjected to rules decreed by the forces of leniency. Although it flourished, it did not directly threaten family harmony. Both geography and social convention kept middle-class women well away from the disreputable districts. As for the prostitutes, supervised and marginalized in their separate world, they occupied the place in the Quebec reality assigned to them by the authorities.

Conclusion

Two decades represent too short a period in which to document profound transformations or significant new directions either in the definition and expression of social norms or in the toleration or repression of behaviour departing from them. Admittedly, these twenty years were hardly tranquil and unchanging. The boom that replaced the post-war slump too quickly gave way to the Great Depression of the 1930s. There was one insecurity after another, and insecurity is the hallmark of the public discourse of this period. Economic uncertainty was a threat to social stability, certainly, but economic prosperity, with its attendant industrial development, population shifts, and exposure to foreign culture also gave rise to anxieties.

In the political arena, there was a single great change at the top – the Union Nationale came to power in Quebec in 1936 after forty years of Liberal rule. But economic policy remained liberal and the civil power continued to perpetuate itself and embrace the same social philosophy. The emergence in these decades of a nationalist ideology, as embodied by Lionel Groulx, l'Action libérale nationale, and other, even more conservative movements, demanded a continued attachment to the vernacular traditions.

The Church, whose beliefs rested on immutable principles, maintained both its values and its prohibitions. Papal encyclicals, responding to contemporary problems, clarified the positions it took but made no concessions to the modern age in the realm of private life.

In these circumstances, despite the material transformations affecting Quebec society, it is not surprising to see the insistence on natalism, on extramarital chastity, and on the essentially maternal role of women. The ideal of Quebec womanhood was fashioned from social and moral assumptions that were virtually seamless, omnipresent, and inflexible. Reforms in civil rights and in social assistance were firmly based on traditional positions. Allowing married women the right to have a bank account of $2,000, or granting benefits to needy mothers, or including women's suffrage in the Liberal Party platform could be accepted if all concerned could be assured that these measures would not affect the fundamental maternal role of women.

There are two indications, however, of how much determination went into imposing the rules used to construct the feminine ideal – the extent of deviant behaviour and the amount of repression exercised to suppress it. Deviance is defined by the social norms but is shaped by the times and the economic and social context in which it is expressed. Evaluating the importance of violations of the code that regulated reproduction and female sexuality is nearly impossible given the hidden nature of acts that are both intimate and private or disguised to a greater or lesser degree, as in the case of prostitution. From official statistics we are able to demonstrate a decrease in the birth rate, which clearly reveals contraceptive use and explains why religious and secular authorities so often condemned these prohibited methods.

As for abortion, neither recorded deaths nor court proceedings give an adequate indication of the real situation. The impressions of the judges and physicians allow us to conclude that the economic hardships of the thirties persuaded a large number of women to terminate their pregnancies. But the cost of an abortion was prohibitive, especially for women who lived far from the larger cities and who had to travel long distances and pay for a place to stay. In these cases, the pregnancy would commonly go to term and the child would be left in a crèche. The numbers of children abandoned, whether in the street or at a crèche, rose during the Great Depression and give an indication of the distress of desperate mothers. Infanticide, that last resort, could be so well disguised that we cannot even guess its extent.

The demographic statistics admittedly underestimate the number of single mothers. "Illegitimate" births always represented less than 4 per cent of the annual births, but their 37 per cent rise between 1931 and 1939,[1] if it does not indicate a relaxation of moral standards, at least suggests the effect of economic hardship that prevented the marriage of pregnant young women. These would in turn swell the numbers of abortions and abandoned children. As for prostitution, neither the arrest records nor the estimates of investigators give a valid idea of its importance in Montreal. The arrests were a result either of public pressure, as in the crackdown of 1923, or of a change in personnel, as with the naming of a new chief of police, Fernand Dufresne, who left his position as recorder in 1931 to "rid Montreal of organized vice."[2] We can, however, have some confidence in the observations of those who noted an upsurge in street prostitution linked to a lack of work immediately after the war and then during the depression ten years later.

As departures from sanctioned behaviour persisted and even increased, repression was pursued more or less vigorously depending on whether the offences were seen to represent a serious threat to the social order. A distinction must be made between official punishment on the part of the authorities and social sanctions, which might be no less harsh, though they were sometimes more subtle. The authorities tolerated more than they repressed. Illegal condoms were available at many locations. However well known they were, the abortionists were not hounded into closing their doors. There was very little effort invested in finding the mothers who had abandoned their babies. Even infanticide was greeted with understanding. Prostitution was viewed with considerable ambiguity. The interests involved in it, from the client to the brothel-keeper, came up against a public opinion from time to time that was aroused by the hypocrisy of the system and by the scandal it provoked. A sense of public outrage spawned these periodic crackdowns, which produced such insubstantial results that no one was deterred for long from pursuing a career in vice. Of all the groups of women studied here, prostitutes were virtually the only ones who regularly came into contact with the forces of law and order and received jail terms, but these were never long enough to prevent them from offending again. Their activities were tolerated as long as they were watched, controlled, and confined within certain limits.

A social stigma might attach to those the authorities overlooked. The voluntary refusal to become a mother was unacceptable but not always detectable. The limitation of the number of children might have been the result of great personal discipline; an abortion might be passed off as a miscarriage. Social disapproval did not prevent women from sharing their secrets and their secret addresses, but these exchanges remained private and were protected by confidentiality.

Single mothers felt the weight of disapproval by the society they were seen to have dishonoured rather than the sanction of the civil authorities, who left them alone. Although those studied at the Hôpital de la Miséricorde came chiefly from among the disadvantaged, they came from every social class and they had to be hidden to avoid scandal. Concealing both their pregnancies and their children allowed these women the possibility of resuming their lives, of becoming reintegrated into the social fabric, so as to be able to get work, find a husband, and start a "legitimate" family. But this new life depended on absolute discretion.

Prostitutes lived at the edge of what was considered normal – they were only accepted in a world that operated by its own rules and values. Treated with contempt by the authorities with whom they came into contact, they nevertheless had their place and formed an integral part of the urban scene.

What was officially said and what was done in practice may appear contradictory. The official position, almost always invariable and inflexible, defined what was seen to be the norm and established what deviant behaviour would be more tolerated, and what less. It is as if, parallel to the norm, there existed an "alternative" standard, one that took human nature and the weakness of the flesh (especially male flesh) into account and responded to familial and material concerns. Contraception, abortion, and prostitution were, for different reasons, responses to social needs.

The kinds of behaviour that were the least permissible were those that represented the greatest threat to the foundations of the family. When economic upheavals were attacking the very structure of the family, social commentators clung to stability and went in full cry after everything that might dilute it. Social deviations, indicators of deep-rooted disorder, became the object of vehement denunciation. But in actual fact, the forces of order did not respond to the concerns of the social elite. For one thing, the number of law enforcement officers was affected by budgetary constraint, as occurred after the First World War. For another, it requires a certain will to employ harsh measures. This willingness was present only sporadically, responding to public pressure and administrative directives. Religious and political elements, anxious to preserve a Quebec society based on a patriarchal conception of the family, reacted with alarm to every economic and social alteration to the family circle. The more the family was threatened, the more anxious they became and the louder their appeal to traditions, especially to the maternal role of women.

These twenty years of economic and social transformation produced public discussion and policies that sought to slow social change and to reinforce traditional female roles. During these twenty years, women who had been defined as deviant remained unrepentant and conducted themselves in ways that were far more accepted than anyone would have dared to admit. They were deviant, but only in relation to a norm upheld in order to stave off the modernism that threatened to swallow up a Quebec based on long-established social and sexual roles.

Notes

Chapter 1

1. This term involves an anachronism, since in the period under discussion the word was applied exclusively to women living in Quebec City. As the language has evolved, the word *Québécoises* now applies to the women of the entire province.
2. Nicole-Claude Mathieu, "Quand céder n'est pas consentir," *L'Arraisonnement des femmes. Essais en anthropologie des sexes.* Cahiers de l'Homme (Paris: École des Hautes Études en Sciences sociales, 1985), p. 230.
3. Guy LaForest, "Le sculpteur collectif et l'État pastoral," *Recherches sociographiques,* 27, 1 (1986), pp. 138, 142. Jean Hamelin and Nicole Gagnon, *Histoire du catholicisme au Québec. Le XXe siècle* I, *1898-1940* (Montréal: Boréal Express, 1984), pp. 41-51.
4. Jean-Louis Flandrin, *Le Sexe et l'Occident. Évolution des attitudes et des comportements* (Paris: Seuil, 1981). Michel Foucault, *Histoire de la sexualité,* vol. I, *La Volonté de savoir* (Paris: NRF Gallimard, 1976). Yvonne Knibiehler and Catherine Fouquet, *La Femme et les Médecins. Analyse historique* (Paris: Hachette, 1983). In addition, there is an entire English and American literature on the subject that is too extensive to note here.
5. Albert Le Sage, "Influence sociale de la presse médicale au Canada," report to the International Congress on "La presse médicale latine" (Venice: 29 September-3 October 1936). *L'Union médicale,* 66, 1 (January, 1937), pp. 4-41. See Andrée Lévesque, "Mères ou malades: les Québécoises de l'entre-deux-guerres vues par les médecins," *Revue d'histoire de l'Amérique française,* 38 (1984), pp. 23-37.
6. Pauline Fréchette-Handfield, "L'art d'être une bonne mère," *La Bonne Parole,* 11, 2 (February, 1923), p. 10.
7. See, for example, the advertisements in *La Revue moderne.*
8. Lévesque, "Mères ou malades," p. 31.

9. Leglius-A. Gagnier, *Droits et devoirs de la médecine et des médecins canadiens-français* (Montréal, 1926).

10. Joseph-Papin Archambault, S.J., "Déclaration d'ouverture," Semaine sociale du Canada, IVe session, *La Famille* (Montréal: Bibliothèque de l'Action française, 1923), pp. 13, 16.

11. Jeanne Anctil, "L'enseignement ménager," *La Famille,* p. 248.

12. Department of Labour, *Le Mouvement syndical ouvrier au Canada* (Ottawa: King's Printers, 1930).

13. Referring to Michel Foucault, Derrida draws a distinction between his history of madness "itself" and a history "about" madness. Jacques Derrida, *L'Écriture et la Différence* (Paris: Seuil, 1967), p. 56.

14. Montreal, Municipal Court Archives, Recorder's Court, The King v. Florida Carroll (26 February 1930), GP 3573.

15. Archives of the Hôpital de la Miséricorde de Montréal (AHM), #35175 (May, 1937).

16. Derrida, *L'Écriture,* p. 11.

17. Geoffrey Ewen, "La contestation à Montréal en 1919," *Bulletin d'Histoire des travailleurs québécois,* RCHTQ, 36 (1986), pp. 37-62.

18. Canada, Federal Bureau of Statistics, *Annuaire du Canada (AC), 1934* (Ottawa: King's Printer, 1935), p. 841.

19. Alexandre Taschereau, "De l'influence de la femme sur nos destinées nationales," a lecture before the FNSJB, April, 1921, *La Bonne Parole,* 9, 5 (May, 1921), pp. 6-9.

20. *La Tribune de Sherbrooke,* 5 March 1931.

21. Archambault, "Déclaration d'ouverture," p. 14.

22. Encyclical *Ubi Arcano,* 11 December 1922, *Lettres et Mandements,* 17, pp. 142-81.

23. Circulaire de Mgr l'Administrateur apostolique au clergé de son diocèse [Open letter from the Apostolic Administrator to the priests of his diocese], no. 13, 25 January 1924, *Lettres et Mandements,* 17, p. 301.

24. Archambault, "Déclaration d'ouverture," p. 13.

25. *Ibid.,* p. 16. "Circulaire du clergé," the Archbishop of Quebec, no. 10, (8 November 1927). *Mandements des évêques de Québec,* 13 (1925-1931), p. 230. Henri Martin, "La dépopulation," *La Famille,* pp. 153-54.

26. Archambault, "Déclaration d'ouverture," p. 16.

27. Graham Lowe, *Women in the Administrative Revolution* (Toronto: University of Toronto Press, 1988).

28. *Le Canada,* 30 March 1926.

29. *La Presse,* 27 February 1931. For the editorial writer, the enemy was communism, which could be resisted by the family.

30. Pastoral letter of His Eminence Raymond Marie Cardinal Rouleau, Archbishop of Quebec, and the archbishops and bishops of the ecclesiastic provinces of Quebec and Ottawa, on divorce, no. 40A (2 February 1930).

Lettres et Mandements, 18. "Circulaire du clergé," no. 34 (December, 1936). *Mandements des évêques de Québec,* 15 (1936-1939).

31. Madame Edmond Brossard, "Causes de la déchéance morale des familles," *La Bonne Parole,* 20, 6 (June, 1932), pp. 1-4.

Chapter 2

1. *La Bonne Parole,* 10, 8 (July-August, 1922), p. 7.
2. Helen MacMurchy, *Le Livre des mères canadiennes* (Ottawa: Minister of Health, 1923), p. 7.
3. R.P. Manisse, *L'Avenir de la jeune fille. Que vais-je faire? Rester fille ou me marier?* (Sainte-Anne-de-Bellevue, 1935), p. 46.
4. *La Presse,* 20 March 1925.
5. *La Patrie,* 27 February, 6 March 1926.
6. Henriette Dessaulles Saint-Jacques ("Fadette"), "L'éducation familiale," *La Famille,* p. 290.
7. Pascale Matte, "Le courrier de Colette," unpublished paper, Department of History, McGill University, 1985.
8. Quoted in Micheline Dumont and Nadia Fahmy-Eid, *Les Couventines. L'éducation des filles au Québec dans les congrégations religieuses enseignantes 1840-1960* (Montréal: Boréal, 1986), p. 59.
9. Sr. Marie Gérin-Lajoie, "Le retour de la mère au foyer," Semaine sociale du Canada, 11th session, *L'Ordre social chrétien* (Montréal: École sociale populaire, 1932), p. 196.
10. Victorin Germain, *Catéchèse de 6e et 9e commandements de Dieu* (Québec, 1938), p. 65.
11. Statistics taken from *Census of Canada,* 1921, 1931, 1941 (Ottawa: King's Printer). Canon Groulx recalled with nostalgia how in New France fathers of "old maids" of more than sixteen and of "old lads" who had reached twenty were "liable to a certain fine." Lionel Groulx, *Notre maître le passé* (Montréal: Granger Frères, 1924), p. 128.
12. Henriette Tassé (Lionais), *De tout et de peu* (Montréal: Cie. d'imprimerie des marchands ltée, 1923), p. 27.
13. Henriette Tassé, *La Femme et la Civilisation* (Montréal: Thérien Frères, 1927), p. 103.
14. Janine Broynard-Frot, *Un matriarcat sans procès. Analyse systématique de romans canadiens-français, 1860-1960* (Montréal: Presse de l'Université de Montréal, 1982).
15. Patricia Smart, *Écrire dans la maison du père. L'émergence du féminin dans la tradition littéraire du Québec* (Montréal: Québec/Amérique, 1988).
16. *Ibid.,* p. 330.
17. L.P. Mercier, *Quoi dire, comment dire et quoi faire. Éducation sexuelle* (Montréal: Fides, 1930), p. 47.
18. "Fadette," "L'éducation familiale," pp. 291-93. See Danielle Nepveu,

"Les loisirs éducatifs," in Dumont and Fahmy-Eid, *Les Couventines,* p. 67.

19. Victorin Germain, *Le Point d'interrogation* (Québec, 1936), p. 49. Flandrin, *Le Sexe et l'Occident,* pp. 101-08.

20. Archbishop of Quebec, "Circulaire du clergé," 10 (8 November 1927), *Mandements des évêques de Québec 13,* 1925-1931, pp. 230-31.

21. Olivier Maurault, P.S.S., "Veillée religieuse," *La Famille,* pp. 310-12.

22. The name of the English economist Robert Malthus (1766-1844) had become associated with contraceptive practices. While he recommended delaying marriage as a means of controlling population, his followers recommended the use of contraceptives.

23. Martin, "La dépopulation," p. 150.

24. *Ibid.,* p. 154. For more on Albert Pinard, see Knibiehler and Fouquet, *La Femme et les Médecins,* pp. 238-239.

25. P. Louis-Marie, O.C.R., *Hérédité* (Oka: La Trappe, 1936), p. 435.

26. Germain, *Le Point d'interrogation,* pp. 57-58.

27. Gaston Lapierre, "La limitation des naissances et les lois de stérilisation," *Annales Médico-chirurgicales de l'hôpital Ste-Justine,* 2, 2 (May, 1935), p. 48.

28. *Montreal Daily Star,* 17 March 1937. For the Eastview trial, see Diane Dodd, "The Canadian Birth Control Movement on Trial, 1936-37," *Histoire sociale/Social History,* 16, 32 (November, 1983), pp. 411-28.

29. Ernest Couture, *La Mère canadienne et son enfant* (Ottawa: Minister of Pensions and National Health, 1942), p. 1.

30. Louis Lalande, S.J., "La revanche des berceaux," *L'Action française,* 2 (1918), p. 99.

31. Archambault, "Déclaration d'ouverture," p. 20.

32. *Le Devoir,* 7 March 1933.

33. *AC,* 1920-1941. Minister of Industry and Commerce, *Annuaire statistique du Québec* (Quebec: King's Printer, 1952).

34. *La Presse,* 4 June 1925.

35. *La Patrie,* 21 February 1928.

36. Henriette Tassé, "Sterilization of the Unfit and Birth Control," p. 7, National Archives of Canada (NAC), Collection of the Montreal Local Council of Women (MLCW), MG28, I164, p. 7. The article is signed Henriette Tassé and bears the note, "Return to Carrie Derick."

37. *La Patrie,* 20 March 1926. Father Germain asserted that, well in advance of medicine, the Church had always made a moral duty of breast-feeding, and he condemned those egotists who shirked the task.

38. Terry Copp, *Classe ouvrière et pauvreté. Les conditions de vie des travailleurs montréalais, 1897-1929* (Montréal: Boréal Express, 1978), pp. 102-08.

39. Dr. J.-A. Beaudoin, "L'ennemi dans la place: la mortalité infantile," *L'Action française,* 11 (January, 1924), p. 7. S.A. Knopf, "Augumentation

alarmante de la morbidité et de la mortalité par tuberculose chez les jeunes femmes," *L'Union médicale,* 57, 8 (August, 1929), pp. 464-70. There had been a long-standing interest in the links between the feeding of babies and infant mortality. See Hubert de la Rue, *De la manière d'élever les enfants* (Québec, 1876). Conseil d'hygiène de la province de Québec, *Sauvons nos petits enfants* (Québec, c. 1906.)

40. Gaston Lapierre, *Pour la mère et l'infirmière, Manuel de puériculture* (Montréal: Édouard Garand, 1931), pp. 15, 33-34.

41. Dr. Joseph Gauvreau, "La mortalité infantile," *La Famille,* pp. 162, 171.

42. Daniel Longpré, "L'alimentation artificielle du nourisson normal," *L'Union médicale,* 68 (July, 1939), pp. 748-50. J.-A. Beaudoin, "La limitation des naissances et les lois de stérilisation," *Annales Médico-chirurgicales de l'hôpital Ste-Justine,* 2, 2 (May, 1935), pp. 42-59. Beaudoin, *Cours d'hygiène* (Montréal: Édition scolaire, 1935).

43. Lapierre, *Pour la mère.*

44. Couture, *La Mère canadienne,* pp. 2, 3, 7, 8, 11, 163, 131. In the same vein, gynecologist Hector Sanche wrote in 1939 that a woman ought not to abandon medical attention until after she delivers because "that physiological condition leads to such modifications in the female organism she has hardly experienced before, that she cannot discriminate between what is normal and what is not." Hector Sanche, "La rançon de la maternité," *L'Union médicale,* 68 (March, 1939), p. 253.

45. Hélène Laforce, *Histoire de la sage-femme dans la région de Québec* (Québec: IQRC, 1985).

46. Beaudoin, *Cours d'hygiène,* p. 501.

47. Gauvreau, "La mortalité infantile," p. 162.

48. *Le Canada,* 10 February 1926.

49. "Circulaire de Mgr. l'Administrateur apostolique au clergé de son diocèse," 13, Archevêché de Montréal (25 January 1924). *Lettres et Mandements,* 17, pp. 313-14.

50. *La Patrie,* 13 March 1925.

51. Mme. Louis-F. Coderre, "Le foyer," Semaine sociale du Canada, 5th session, *La Propriété* (Montréal: Bibliothèque de l'Action française, 1924), pp. 139-49. Her attitude sheds some light on the theory of "domestic feminism" developed by certain feminists of the previous decade. It was a theory that ignored the legal, political, and economic inferiority of women and the inequality of real power even in the domestic sphere. The moral power of women, dependent on the good will of the males who called the shots, in no way compensated for their inferior status in the public sphere, where decisions are actually made.

52. Gérin-Lajoie, "Le retour," pp. 196-97, 205-12.

53. *Arcanum Divinae Sapientiae,* Les enseignements pontificaux, *Le Problème féminin,* présentation et tables par les moines de Solesme (Tournai: Desclée, 1953), p. 4.

54. Cyrille Gagnon, "La constitution de la famille," *La Famille,* p. 33.
55. L. Cadieux, *École sociale populaire,* brochure 217-218, 1932, pp. 27-28. Cited in Gilles Routhier, "L'ordre du monde capitaliste et communiste dans la doctrine de l'École sociale populaire 1930-1936," *Recherches sociographiques,* 22, 1 (January-April, 1981), pp. 38-39.
56. Dominique-Augustin Turcotte, *Pour restaurer le foyer* (Montréal, 1940), p. 76.
57. "Le foyer domestique et l'instruction ménagère," *La Bonne Parole,* 14, 12 (December, 1926), pp. 4-5.
58. Turcotte, *Pour restaurer le foyer,* pp. 75, 223-24.
59. MacMurchy, *Le Livre des mères,* pp. 13-14, 78-79, 153.
60. Mgr. Louis-Adolphe Paquet, "L'influence maternelle," lecture given in Jacques Cartier, Quebec (1928). *Études et Appréciations.* Nouveaux thèmes sociaux (Québec: Imprimerie franciscaine missionaire, 1932), p. 122.
61. L.-A. Paquet, "Le féminisme," *Le Canada français,* 1, 4 (December, 1919), p. 233.
62. Paquet, "Le féminisme," *Le Canada français,* 2, 1 (February, 1919), pp. 7, 13, 14, 20. In 1922 he repeated his arguments from nature in "Le vote des femmes," *Études et appréciations* (1922), pp. 315-23.
63. This appears in a pastoral letter on "The Religious Conditions of Canadian Society" [Conditions religieuse de la Societé canadienne] (8 July 1920). Paquet, "Le vote," p. 323.
64. Alphonse Désilets, "Les cercles des fermières dans le province de Québec," Semaine sociale du Canada, 8th session, *Le Problème économique* (Montréal: ACJC, 1928), p. 178.
65. Tassé, *La Femme et la Civilisation,* p. 109.
66. *Le Monde ouvrier,* 4 April 1925.
67. *Le Monde ouvrier,* 14 June 1930. Gustave Francq was surely protecting male jobs when he wrote, "You will agree with me that the natural role of women, especially married women, is to remain in the home." (19 January 1935).
68. Canada. *Recensement du Canada 1931,* vol. VII (Ottawa: King's Printer, 1936), table 26, p. 37.

Percentage of the Female Population over 15 in Paid Employment

	Quebec		Canada	
	1921	1931	1921	1931
Single	42.83%	46.72%	42.09%	46.58%
Married	1.81	2.88	2.16	3.45
Widowed & divorced	22.86	20.94	21.65	21.03

69. *Vie ouvrière* came out between 1932 and 1934 and should not be confused with *Vie ouvrière,* published from 1950.

70. Henri Bourassa, *Le Divorce. Aspects constitutionnels et politiques.* Causerie au Cercle universitaire de Montréal, 12 April 1930 (Montréal: Imprimerie du Devoir, 1930), pp. 17-18.

71. *La Patrie,* 1 June 1923.

72. Charles-Émile le Bruchési, "Les bases juridiques de la famille," *La Famille,* p. 237. "Les naissances baissent partout où les divorces montent," Martin, "La dépopulation," p. 149.

73. Canada. *Débats, Chambre des Communes,* IV (26 February 1925), pp. 554-55; (4 June 1925), p. 3853. *Débats, Sénat* (10 June 1925), p. 431.

74. M. Letellier, the member from Compton, spoke in opposition to J.S. Woodsworth's bill in order to prevent the spread of a social evil. *Débats, Chambre des Communes* (10 March 1930).

75. Lettre pastorale de S. Em. le cardinal Raymond Marie Rouleau, archevêque de Québec et des archevêques et évêques des provinces ecclésiastiques de Québec et d'Ottawa, sur le divorce (Pastoral letter from His Eminence Raymond Marie Cardinal Rouleau, Archbishop of Quebec and the archbishops and bishops of the ecclesiastical provinces of Quebec and Ottawa, on divorce) 40A (2 February 1930), *Lettres et Mandements,* p. 18.

76. C.E. Dorion, "L'État et le mariage," Semaine sociale du Canada, 10th session, *L'État* (Montréal: École sociale populaire, 1931), pp. 188-89.

77. Flandrin, *Le Sexe et l'Occident,* pp. 116-17.

78. See Angus McLaren and Arlene Tigar McLaren, *The Bedroom and the State: The Changing Practices and Politics of Contraception and Abortion in Canada, 1880-1980* (Toronto: McClelland and Stewart, 1986), p. 9. According to the historian John T. Noonan, by the 1880s the Vatican had already accepted a rhythm method based on the menstrual cycle. *Contraception: A History of its Treatment by Catholic Theologians and Canonists* (Cambridge, Mass.: Harvard University Press, 1965), pp. 441-42.

79. Québec, Ministère de la justice (Centre de préarchivage), District of Montreal (MJDM), Bugeaud v. Cherry, Sessions Court (1938), GP 10079, Court of the King's Bench (1938), p. 335.

80. Grisez, *Abortion,* p. 180.

81. Hervé Trudel, *Éléments de morale médicale* (Montréal: Granger Frères, 1928), p. 20.

82. Germain, *Le Point,* pp. 52-54.

83. *Semaine religieuse de Montréal,* 98, 28 (12 July 1939), p. 444.

84. Constance Backhouse, "Involuntary Motherhood: Abortion, Birth Control and the Law in Nineteenth Century Canada," *Windsor Yearbook of Access to Justice,* 3 (1983), pp. 75-76.

85. *La Presse,* 20 February 1931.

86. Recorder's Court was "charged with punishing infractions of police or municipal regulations." *ASQ* (1931), pp. 156-57.

87. NAC, MG28, I129, 2. *Le Devoir,* 30 January 1933.

88. Graziella Boissonnault, "La pension aux mères," *La Bonne Parole,* 10, 1 (January, 1922), pp. 4, 15; no. 9 (September, 1927), p. 11.

89. Commission sur les affaires sociales, *Deuxième Rapport* (January, 1934), p. 34.

90. Léon Lebel, S.J., *Les Allocations familiales,* Tracts 159-160 (Montréal: École sociale populaire, 1927). *Pourquoi les allocations familiales? Raisons et objections* (Montréal: Arbour et Dupont, 1928). *Le problème de la famille nombreuse. Sa solution. Les allocations familiales* (Montréal).

91. Lebel, *Le problème,* pp. 9, 25.

92. Émile Clouthier, "Le salaire et le famille," Semaine sociale du Canada, Third session, *Capital et travail* (Ottawa, 1922); (Montréal: Bibliothèque de l'Action française, 1923), p. 162.

93. Hermas Bastien, "Pour la famille nombreuse," *L'Action française,* 17 (August, 1927), p. 118.

94. Georges-Marie Bilodeau, *Le Vrai Remède. Étude sur la crise actuelle. Remèdes proposés* (Québec: L'Action sociale ltée, 1931), pp. 91-92.

95. *Le Devoir,* 16 March 1921.

96. *L'Union médicale,* 61 (1932), p. 1157.

97. Québec. *Statuts de la Province de Québec* (17 April 1937), session 2, 20th Legislature, I Geo. VI, chap. 81.

98. For an account of the battle waged by Quebec women to have the payments issued in their names, like all other Canadian women, see Thérèse Casgrain, *Une femme chez les hommes* (Montréal: Éditions du Jour, 1971), pp. 170-74. Simonne Monet-Chartrand, *Ma Vie comme rivière,* II (Montréal: Éditions du remue-ménage, 1982), pp. 256-57.

99. Beaudoin, *Cours d'hygiene,* pp. 15, 18-19.

100. Lapierre, "La limitation," p. 101.

101. Ferdinand Roy, "L'autorité dans la famille," Semaine sociale du Canada, 7th session, *L'Autorité* (Montréal: Bibliothèque de l'Action française, 1927), pp. 61-63.

102. *La Presse,* 6 April 1925.

103. "Fadette," "L'éducation familiale," p. 289.

104. *Le Canada,* 16, 18 February 1928.

105. *La Presse,* 24 July 1939; *La Patrie,* 24 July 1939. Eric Hutton, "The Happy Sequel to Quebec's Great Ballpark Wedding," *Maclean's,* 6 December 1958, pp. 35-36.

106. Clio Collective, *L'Histoire des femmes au Québec depuis quatre siècles* (Montréal: Quinze, 1982), p. 262.

107. "L'assistance maternelle," *La Bonne Parole,* 15, 9 (September, 1927), p. 8.

108. "L'assistance maternelle," *La Bonne Parole,* 10 (May, 1922), p. 5.

109. *La Bonne Parole,* 15, 9 (September, 1927), p. 9. *La Presse,* 8 April 1925. *La Patrie,* 20 February 1934.

110. See Nicole Thivierge, *Écoles ménagères et instituts familiaux: un modèle féminin traditionnel* (Québec: IQRC, 1982). Marie Lacoste Gérin-Lajoie observed that the domestic science inspectors in the schools were men. *Le Devoir,* 8 March 1922.

111. Marie Lacoste Gérin-Lajoie, "Le 25e anniversaire de la fondation de la FNSJB," *La Bonne Parole,* 20, 5 (May, 1932).

112. Of 6,853 women enrolled, 1,401 dropped out, while only 315 out of 13,542 men failed to finish their program. Department of Labour, *Training Canada's Young Unemployed. Facts, Figures, and Objectives of the Dominion-Provincial Youth Training Programme* (Ottawa: King's Printer, 1938), pp. 16, 18, 24.

113. Henri Bourassa, *Femmes-Hommes ou Hommes et Femmes? Étude à bâtons rompus sur le féminisme* (Montréal: Imprimerie du Devoir, 1925), p. 77.

114. *Le Devoir,* 1 April 1918. Bourassa was quoted most approvingly by Paquet in "Le féminisme," pp. 2, 16. For an account of Bourassa's views on feminism, see Susan Mann Trofimenkoff, "Henri Bourassa and the 'Woman Question'," *Journal of Canadian Studies,* 10 (November, 1975), pp. 3-11.

115. See Arthur Trahan's speech on women's suffrage, Ottawa, 11 April 1918.

116. Canada, *Débats, Chambre des Communes,* I (11 April 1918), p. 638.

117. "Fadette," "L'éducation familiale," p. 290.

118. See Lévesque, "Mères ou malades."

119. *Le Canada,* 22 February 1934.

120. *Le Canada,* 21 March 1935.

121. *La Bonne Parole,* 9, 5 (May, 1921), pp. 6-9.

122. Such was the experience of the match-makers in their 1925 strike. Michelle Lapointe, "Le syndicat catholique des allumettières de Hull, 1919-1924," *RHAF,* 32, 4 (March, 1979), pp. 603-28.

123. *Montreal Daily Star,* 22 December 1933.

124. *La Femme canadienne-française. Almanach de la langue française,* ed. Albert Lévesque (Montréal, 1936), p. 14.

Chapter 3

1. Manisse, *L'Avenir de la jeune fille,* p. 4.

2. Statistics Canada, *Census of Canada,* 1921, II, table 29. The number of Quebec women in religious communities was 20,021 in 1920, 26,468 in 1930, and 33,031 in 1939. Nicole Laurin, Danielle Juteau, and Lorraine Duchesne, *A la Recherche d'un monde oublié. Les communautés religieuses de femmes au Québec de 1900 à 1970* (Montréal: Le Jour, 1991), pp. 411-12.

3. Manisse, *L'Avenir de la jeune fille*, p. 20.

4. Germain, *Catéchèse*, p. 125.

5. René de Cotret, *Soeur ou fiancée* (Montréal, 1932), p. 19.

6. *La Bonne Parole*, 7, 2 (April, 1919), pp. 2-7.

7. Arthur Saint-Pierre, *L'oeuvre des congrégations religieuses de charité dans le province de Québec en 1930* (Montréal: Éditions de la Bibliothèque canadienne, 1930), p. 157.

8. Jovette Bernier, *La Chair décevante* (Montréal, 1931). In a review of the work, Jean Bruchési attacked the immorality of the novel and considered the heroine to be "ripe for Bolshevism." Jean Bruchési, "Le Monde des lettres," *La Revue moderne*, 18 (February, 1932).

9. de Cotret, *Soeur ou fiancée*, pp. 45-46, 51.

10. Bernier, *La Chair décevante*, pp. 29-33. Concealment could not altogether erase the long-term consequences of youthful error. In an era aware of heredity and eugenics, both authors imagine the possibility of an intermarriage when their heroine's son falls in love with his half-sister, that is, with the daughter of his biological father. It turns out to be a case of mistaken identity in de Cotret's novel, but Jovette Bernier locks her heroine up in Saint-Jean-de-Dieu Hospital for the mentally ill.

11. Canada, *Débats, Sénat*, 10 June 1925, pp. 432, 433.

12. *La Patrie*, 21 January 1932. In Quebec, young men's sexual exploits were not always met with open indulgence. In a work intended for their benefit, a single standard of morality based on abstinence was advocated on the grounds that every act of fornication involved both sexes. Dr. Douglas White, *Lettre ouverte aux jeunes gens* (Montréal: Édition de la Ligue canadienne de santé), pp. 8-9.

13. Mgr. Bruchési, Pastoral Letter, "Sur les maux de l'heure présente," *Lettres et Mandements*, 16, pp. 358-71.

14. La Revue Dominicaine, *Notre américanisation* (Montréal: L'oeuvre de Presse dominicaine, 1937). For an analysis of this phenomenon, see Odette Vincent-Domey, "L'Américaine: 'la pire des infiltrations étrangères'? 1880-1936," unpublished paper, Department of History, University of Ottawa, 1986.

15. *La Bonne Parole*, 14, 9 (September, 1927), p. 6.

16. "Circulaire au clergé," no. 52 (31 December 1938). Decrees and ordinances appearing in *Semaine religieuse, Mandements des évêques de Québec, 1936-39*, XV, p. 469.

17. *Le Monde ouvrier*, 15, 9 (September, 1927), p. 6.

18. "Circulaire de Mgr. l'Administrateur apostolique au clergé de son diocèse," no. 13 (25 January 1924), *Lettres et Mandements*, 17, p. 305. "Lettre pastorale de N.S. l'Archevêque de Québec et les Évêques de la Province ecclésiastique de Québec sur le fléchissement de la moralité et le naturalisme de la vie," no. 5 (2 February 1927), *Mandements des évêques*

de Québec, XIII, p. 189. "Circulaire au clergé," Archevêque de Québec, no. 24 (8 December 1929), pp. 489-90; 28 September 1935, XLVI, p. 492.

19. "Lettre pastorale . . . sur le fléchissement de la moralité," p. 189.

20. "Circulaire au clergé," no. 7 (31 December 1931), appearing in *Semaine religieuse,* "Plages et bains publics" (16 June 1932), *Lettres et Mandements . . . 1925-1935,* 4, pp. 97-98.

21. *La Bonne Parole,* 21 June 1939.

22. "Circulaire au clergé," 31 December 1938, p. 482.

23. "Lettre pastorale . . . sur le fléchissement de la moralité," p. 193.

24. *Ibid.,* p. 188.

25. Victor Margueritte, *La Garçonne* (Paris: Flammarion, 1921).

26. Georges Panneton, *Le Garçonnisme* (Québec: Semaine religieuse de Québec, 1932), pp. 10, 14, 17.

27. Claire Martin, *Dans un gant de fer* (Montréal: Le Cercle du livre de France, 1965), pp. 98, 113, 175.

28. Germain, *Catéchèse,* p. 61.

29. Victorin Germain, *Les Récits de la crèche* (Québec: n.p., n.d.), pp. 60, 62.

30. *Montreal Standard,* 21 April 1923.

31. *La Bonne Parole,* 19, 9 (September, 1931). The white slave trade phobia persisted for a long time in Quebec. In his story "Voleur de filles," Father Germain tells the tale of a young country girl who, on the train that is bringing her to the city, is hired by a couple who introduce her to "looseness, emancipation, and depravity." She takes refuge at the Hôpital de la Miséricorde, where the nuns find her a good home, but not without the taxi-driver's bringing her to a house where they were "dancing, drinking, and playing cards," instead of to her intended destination. The moral? "Good and decent country girls, stay home where you belong!" Germain, *Les Récits,* p. 15.

32. *Le Monde ouvrier,* 25 January 1919.

33. L.M. Pautrier, *Résumé de cours de perfectionnement en dermato-vénérologie et urologie* (Montréal: Beauchemin, 1923), pp. 115-16.

34. Montréal, *Commission d'enquête sur le Service de Police de Montréal* (hereafter Coderre Commission) 1924-25, Desloges, vol. 8, p. 7841.

35. For Dr. A.-H. Desloges, "it is easy to comprehend that a fallen girl is a sullied girl." Coderre Commission, vol. 7, p. 7874.

36. C.M. Derick, "Baby Welfare Exhibit," 12-17 May 1919 NAC, MG 28, I 164 I.

37. *Montreal Herald,* 7 May 1919. Haywood, Coderre Commission, p. 8236. J.-A. Beaudoin, *La Mission sociale de l'hygiène* (Montréal: École sociale populaire, 1928), p. 24.

38. Derick, "Baby Welfare Exhibit."

39. Nathan Gordon, Coderre Commission, vol. 6, p. 6646.

40. A. Gautier, *ibid.,* vol. 2, p. 984.

41. Joseph Tremblay, *ibid.,* vol. 6, p. 6236; Desloges, vol. 7, p. 7886.

42. *Le Monde ouvrier,* 1 March 1919, 22 March 1926.

43. Roderick Stewart, *Bethune* (Markham, Ontario: Paperjacks, 1975), p. 55.

44. J.M.E. Prévost, *Que chacun devrait savoir. Comment prévenir et guérir le mal vénérien et les maladies urinaires,* 2nd edition (Montréal, 1922), p. 12. The prostitute here is the extreme example of the polluted woman, and it is only a short step from her to view women as impure by reason of their physiology – any woman can infect. Menstrual blood has long been the object of religious and medical prohibitions. Dr. Prévost (p. 68) invokes "Mosaic law, which forbids all sexual connection during the menstrual period . . . in order to avoid gonorrhea."

45. Coderre Commission, vol. 8, pp. 7853, 7859, 8083, 8245.

46. Leglius-A. Gagnier, *Droits et devoirs de la médecine et les médicins canadiens-français* (Montréal, 1926), pp. 30-32.

47. Coderre Commission, vol. 8, p. 7632.

48. Jennifer Stoddart, "Quand les gens de robe se penchent sur les droits des femmes: le cas de la commission Dorion, 1929-1931," in Marie Lavigne and Yolande Pinard, *Travailleuses et féministes* (Montréal: Boréal Express, 1983), pp. 328, 331.

49. Canada, *Débats, Chambre des Communes,* 5 July 1919, pp. 4798-99.

50. Canada, *Code criminel,* 1892, 55 and 56 Vict., c. 29, art. 269, pp. 181-84. James G. Snell, "'The White Life for Two': The Defense of Marriage and Sexual Morality in Canada, 1890-1914," *Histoire sociale/Social History,* 16, 31 (May, 1983), p. 121.

51. MDJM, Cour du Banc du Roi and Cour de sessions, 1930-39.

52. MDJM, especially GP 20 660, 1934; GP 2018, 1932.

53. The accused, aged thirty-two, was found not guilty of having seduced his sixteen-year-old girlfriend. GP 2574, 1938. A rape victim who was attacked by five young men and raped by two of them could not win her case probably because the accused claimed that she was not a virgin at the time. The verdict of not guilty demonstrates the futility of pursuing a case when the plaintiff did not testify.

54. Criminal Code, articles 281-283. See John McLaren, "White Slavers: The Reform of Canada's Prostitution Laws and Patterns of Enforcement, 1900-1920," *Criminal Justice History,* 8 (1987), pp. 53-119.

55. Quebec, *Statuts de la Province de Québec,* 1920, 10 Géo. V, Chap. 81, pp. 265-67. See Geoffrion, Coderre Commission, vol. 8, pp. 7719-23, for the difficulties in enforcing this law.

56. *Statuts refondus de la Province de Québec,* Chap. 186, sec. 7, 8, 9, pp. 2353-54.

57. Coderre Commission, vol. 2, p. 988.

58. APC, *Minutes,* 18 March, 13 April 1925, MG28 I164, I.

59. Coderre Commission, vol. 8, pp. 7455-7790. *Le Monde ouvrier,* 1 March

1917, 16 March 1919, 3 January 1925, 22 May 1926, and, 9, 16, 20, 23 April 1932.

60. J.A. Ranger, "La campagne anti-vénérienne," *L'Union médicale*, 50 (November, 1921), pp. 446-47. A.H. Desloges and J.H. Ranger, "Historique de la lutte anti-vénérienne dans la Province de Québec," *L'Union médicale*, 61 (1932), pp. 235-36. Albert LeSage, "La répression de la syphilis," radio discussion, 14 January 1940. In 1929, seventy-one clinics were funded by the government and 38,000 cases received 209,000 treatments. Desloges, *La Tribune de Sherbrooke*, 5 March 1931. J. Cassel, *The Secret Plague* (Toronto: University of Toronto Press, 1987), pp. 194-201, 266-67.

61. Geoffrion, Coderre Commission, vol. 7, p. 7611.

62. Montreal, *Rapport annuel du Service de Police,* 1921-39. See table 4.

63. *Acta A. Sedis,* XXIII, 118, 1931, cited in P. Louis-Marie, *Hérédité. Manuel de génétique* (Oka: Institut agricole d'Oka, La Trappe, 1936), p. 419.

64. Committee of Sixteen, Second Report, *Some Facts Regarding Toleration, Regulation, Segregation, and Repression of Commercialized Vice,* pub. no. 2, (Montreal, 21 February 1919), p. 8.

65. At the Coderre Commission, the president of the executive committee of the city of Montreal, J.A.A. Brodeur, directly credited the Committee of Sixteen with the law against brothel proprietors. Coderre Commission, vol. 6, p. 5919.

66. Andrée Lévesque, "Putting it out: efforts to extinguish the Red Light in Montreal," paper presented to the annual meeting of the Canadian Historical Association, 1987.

67. *La Bonne Parole,* 11, 1 (January, 1923), p. 4.

68. *Ibid.,* 10, 5 (May, 1922), pp. 12-13.

69. "Rapport de la Commission royale chargée de faire enquête sur l'incendie du 'Laurier Palace' et certaines autres matières d'intérêt général," *Documents de la Session,* LXI, no. 50, p. 27, in Michel Prévost, "L'incendie du Laurier Palace," unpublished manuscript, Department of History, University of Ottawa, 26 January 1979.

70. Philippe Perrier, "Contre le cinéma," *L'Action française* (February, 1927), p. 85.

71. A. Harbour, "L'Enquête sur le cinéma," *Semaine religieuse de Montréal,* 45 (26 May 1927), p. 325.

72. "Rapport 'Laurier Palace,'" p. 31, in M. Prévost.

73. "Circulaire du clergé," no. 44 (31 December 1937), in *Semaine religieuse,* 27, "Ligue catholique du cinéma" (23 September 1937). *Lettres et Mandements . . . 1936-1939,* 15, p. 363.

74. Jean-Charles Harvey, *Les Demi-Civilisés* (Montréal: L'Actuelle, 1970).

75. Rinette, "Une Visite au 'Foyer,'" *Le Foyer,* 8 (January, 1911), pp. 129-32. See as well *Le Foyer,* 14, 1 (July, 1916), p. 14.

76. *La Bonne Parole,* 10, 11 (November, 1922), pp. 7-8.
77. Iris, "Conseils à une voyageuse," *Le Foyer,* 14, 12 (June, 1917), pp. 204-05. A.D., "Enquête," *Le Foyer,* 15, 9 (March, 1918), pp. 167-68.
78. *Le Devoir,* 4 February 1933.
79. *La Bonne Parole,* 27, 5 (March, 1938), p. 10; nos. 7-8 (July-August, 1938), p. 22.
80. *Répertoire des Oeuvres sociales de Montréal* (Montréal, 1946), pp. 24, 25, 33.
81. Andrée Lévesque, "Deviant Anonymous: Single Mothers at the Hôpital de la Miséricorde in Montreal, 1929-1939," *Communications historiques/Historical Papers,* Canadian Historical Association (1984), pp. 168-84. See also Marta Danylewycz, *Profession: religieuse. Un choix pour les Québécoises, 1840-1920* (Montréal: Boréal Express, 1988).

Chapter 4

1. "A natural difference only becomes a social difference when the culture demands it." Madeleine Ouellette-Michalska, *L'Amour de la carte postale* (Montréal: Québec-Amérique, 1987), p. 15.
2. Peter Gay, *The Bourgeois Experience: Victoria to Freud.* Vol. I, *Education of the Senses* (New York: Oxford University Press, 1984), pp. 56-58, 458-59. Jeffrey Weeks, *Sex, Politics and Society: The Regulation of Sexuality Since 1800* (London and New York: Longman, 1981), pp. 57-59, 92.
3. Bill McCarthy and John Hagan, "Gender, Delinquency, and the Great Depression: a test of power-control theory," *Canadian Review of Sociology and Anthropology,* 24, 2 (1987), pp. 153-73.
4. James Huzel, "The Incidence of Crime in Vancouver During the Great Depression," in Robert A.J. McDonald and Jean Barman, *Vancouver Past: Essays in Social History* (Vancouver: University of British Columbia Press, 1986), pp. 211-48.
5. See Michel Foucault, *Surveiller et punir. Naissance de la prison* (Paris: Gallimard, NRF, 1975).
6. Thomas Szasz, *The Manufacture of Madness* (New York: Harper & Row, 1970), pp. 16, 191.
7. Kai T. Erikson, "On the Sociology of Deviance," in James F. Davis and Richard Stivers, eds., *The Collective Definition of Deviance* (New York: Free Press, 1975), p. 16.
8. Province de Québec, *Rapports annuels du ministère de la Santé et du Bien-être pour les années 1935-1941* (Québec, 1944), p. 204.
9. *ASQ,* 1933. See table 2.
10. Elsa Gidlow, *I Come with My Songs: The Autobiography of Elsa Gidlow* (San Francisco: Bootlegger Press, 1986).
11. Lynne Chamberland is preparing a doctoral dissertation in sociology on Montreal lesbians.

Chapter 5

1. Marie Lavigne, "Reflexions féministes autour de la fertilité des Québécoises," in Nadia Fahmy-Eid and Micheline Dumont, *Maîtresses de maison. maîtresses d'école* (Montréal: Boréal Express, 1983), p. 325.

2. McLaren and McLaren, *The Bedroom and the State,* pp. 11, 18.

3. Jacques Henripin, *Tendances et facteurs de la fécondité au Canada. Monographie sur le recensement de 1961* (Ottawa: Federal Bureau of Statistics, 1968), p. 21.

4. McLaren and McLaren, *The Bedroom and the State,* pp. 116-24. Diane Dodd, "The Canadian Birth Control Movement on Trial, 1936-1937," *Histoire sociale/Social History,* 16 (November 1983), pp. 411-28.

5. McLaren and McLaren, *The Bedroom and the State,* p. 173.

6. See the trial of Jack Cherry, ch. 6.

7. Bugeaud v. Noël (1935), MJDM, Sessions Court, GP 1326.

8. Coroner v. Viau (1934), GP 8622, 7776.

9. This study is based on the records of thirty-one cases, of which twenty-two are drawn from the Minister of Justice's archives for Sessions Court and the Court of King's Bench, 1919-39, five from the archives of the Hôpital de la Miséricorde, three reports in *L'Union médicale,* and two in the Montreal newspapers.

10. Laberge v. Deniger (1937), GP 11141. Dr. Léon Gérin-Lajoie, "Avortement provoqué, suivi de septicémie suraiguë," *L'Union médicale,* 6/5 (May, 1933), p. 435.

11. Pollinsky v. Brunet (1930), GP 1076. St-Cyr v. Moquin (1934), GP 21202.

12. Coroner v. Viau (1937), GP 8622. Bugeaud v. Bélec (1938), GP 10690, CBR 346.

13. Dr. Léon Gérin-Lajoie, "Césarienne itérative compliquée de rupture utérine quelques minutes avant l'intervention," *L'Union médicale,* 64, 12 (December, 1935), pp. 1414-16.

14. Coderre Commission, vol. 6, p. 5181.

15. *Montreal Daily Star,* 22 March 1923. *La Presse,* 29 May 1925. MJDM, Bugeaud v. Labonté (1930), GP 10753.

16. Dr. O.A. Cannon, "Septic Abortions," *Journal of the Canadian Medical Association,* 12 (March, 1922), p. 163.

17. Gérin-Lajoie, "Avortement provoqué," p. 435.

18. Canada, *Rapports annuels sur la statistique de la criminalité,* Table I: Crimes subject to Jury Trial by Judicial District, *Documents de la Session,* 12 Geo. V (Ottawa: Federal Bureau of Statistics, 1919-1940). Federal, provincial, and municipal statistics vary considerably. From 1928 to 1939, the federal bureau recorded sixty-six charges and fifty convictions. During the same period, l'*Annuaire statistique du Québec* records forty-five convictions ("Condamnations pour crimes et délits graves, par catégories et offenses dans la province de Québec," *ASQ,* 1928-1939).

19. Montreal, *Rapports annuels du service de la police (RASP)*, 1919-1939. The report for 1930 is incomplete and that for 1931 is missing. The statistics are not consistent even with these reports. The summary of crimes, offences, and infractions totals thirty arrests for abortion between 1919 and 1939.

20. de Cotret, *Soeur ou fiancée*, p. 39.

21. Bernier, *La Chair décevante*, p. 142.

22. Cannon, "Septic Abortions," p. 166.

23. Couture, *La Mère canadienne*, p. 44.

24. J.T. Phair and A.H. Sellers, "A Study of Maternal Deaths in the Province of Ontario," *Canadian Public Health Journal (CPHJ)*, 20 (1934), pp. 563-79. F.W. Jackson and R.D. Jeffries, "A Five-Year Study of Maternal Mortality in Manitoba, 1928-1932," *CPHJ*, 25 (1934), p. 97. For a discussion of the methodological problems in estimating the number of abortions, see Arlene Tigar McLaren and Angus McLaren, "Discoveries and Dissimulations: The Impact of Abortion Debate on Maternal Mortality in British Columbia," *B.C. Studies*, 64 (Winter, 1984-85). Seventeen per cent represents a minimum estimate. A study of 717 puerperal mortalities in Philadelphia between 1931 and 1933 indicates that in 39 per cent of deaths abortion was the chief cause of maternal mortality. "Maternal Mortality in Philadelphia," reported in *CPHJ*, 26 (January, 1935), pp. 49-50.

25. Quebec, Provincial Health Service, *12e Rapport annuel* (1933-34), p. 64.

26. Bugeaud v. Noël (1935), Sessions Court, GP 1326.

27. Laurendeau v. Willie et Lachapelle (1929), GP 2699; Bugeaud v. Leclairc (1934), GP 21 738.

28. Bugeaud v. Labonté (1930), GP 10753.

29. Bugeaud v. Noël (1935), Sessions Court, GP 1326. Bugeaud v. Lalanne (1931), GP 1241.

30. Sums based on fourteen cases in Sessions Court in which the amounts dispersed were mentioned.

31. Coroner v. Noël (1936), GP 18109.

32. Bugeaud v. Noël (1935), GP 1326.

33. Cantin v. Deschamps (1933), GP 1326.

34. Dr. Guy D'Argencourt, "Un fait clinique de gynécologie," *L'Union médicale*, 64, 1 (January, 1935), pp. 36-37.

35. Bugeaud v. Moquin (1934), GP 20 956; St. Cyr v. Moquin (1934), GP 21202.

36. MJDM, Sessions Court, Court of King's Bench, 1929-1939.

37. L. Bélec, fifty-four, convinced the court that she used the twigs seized in her home to bring on her periods, since menopause was making her ill. Bugeaud v. Bélec (1938), GP 10690.

38. More than one autopsy reported "a recent pregnancy apparently interrupted by procedures or manoeuvres which are impossible for the doctor to determine." Coroner v. Viau (1934), GP 8622.

39. J.-R. Mercier had been acquitted of infanticide in 1922, charged with abortion in 1925, with murder in 1926, acquitted of abortion in 1937, and finally sentenced to fifteen years for another abortion the same year. All told, three women are known to have died as a result of his activities. Thérrien v. Mercier (1937), GP 11609, and Lamoureaux v. Mercier (1937), GP 4381. *La Patrie* (31 March 1938). Dumontier had already been charged with abortion and acquitted in 1916. Bugeaud v. Dumontier (1938). Noël faced three different charges of abortion or murder in 1935 and 1936 and was sentenced to five years for just one of these crimes. Coroner v. Noël (1936), GP 18109, Bugeaud v. Noël (1935), GP 1326, Bugeaud v. Noël (1935), GP 15270. A. Pettigrew, "Septicémie post-abortum à staphylocoques blancs," *L'Union médicale,* 67 (1938), pp. 256-59.

40. British and American medical literature suggests that the majority of women having recourse to abortion were married. McLaren and McLaren, *The Bedroom and the State,* p. 40; Backhouse, "Involuntary Motherhood," pp. 109-10.

41. Backhouse, "Involuntary Motherhood," pp. 114-15.

42. Kristin Luker, *Abortion and the Politics of Motherhood* (Berkeley: University of California Press, 1984), p. 39.

43. Coroner v. Noël (1936), GP 18109; Bugeaud v. Leclairc (1934), GP 21738; St. Cyr v. Moquin (1934), GP 21202.

44. Luker maintains that, unlike other medical-social questions of the period – slavery, alcoholism, venereal disease, prostitution – only abortion permitted doctors to appear to be motivated by the saving of lives. Luker, *Abortion,* p. 31. See also Backhouse, "Involuntary Motherhood," pp. 78-79.

45. Laberge v. Deniger (1937), GP 11141. On another occasion, the police paid $75 to a pregnant young woman and her sister to ask for an abortion at a house known to the police. Since no abortion took place, no crime could be proved to the Court's satisfaction. Laurendeau v. Willie et Lachapelle (1929), GP 2699.

46. Backhouse, "Involuntary Motherhood," pp. 62-76.

47. de Cotret, *Soeur ou fiancée,* p. 39.

48. Backhouse also notes that in Ontario between 1840 and 1900, there was not a single prosecution of an aborting woman. She sees this fact as reflecting the fundamental concern of doctors to eliminate the competition. Backhouse, "Involuntary Motherhood," pp. 83-85.

49. Constance Backhouse, "Desperate Women and Compassionate Courts: Infanticide in Nineteenth Century Canada," *University of Toronto Law Journal* (1984), pp. 447-55. Criminal code: An Act respecting Offences against the Person (1869), 32 & 33 Vict., c. 20, s. 1, 61, 62.

50. *Le Canada,* 7 March 1930.

51. It does not do to exaggerate the extent of infanticide in the Middle Ages and Renaissance. Far from being normal practice, this crime, which primarily affected "illegitimate" children, was punished very severely. Keith

Wrightson, "Infanticide in European History," *Criminal Justice History,* 3 (1982), pp. 1-3, 14-16.

52. *Le Canada,* 3 January 1923.

53. *La Presse,* 26 March 1931.

54. *La Presse,* 9 February 1931. MDJM, GP 9386, 1931.

55. GP 751, 1936.

56. Coroner v. Delisle (1939), GP 6111.

57. Coroner v. Vinet (1937), GP 5301, CBR 143.

58. *La Patrie,* 26 March 1923. In 1930, a baby was found in the ladies' room at St. Joseph's Oratory. Its parents could not be discovered. *Montreal Herald,* 8 May 1930.

59. *Le Canada,* 22 February 1933.

60. Montreal children found and placed in orphanages for the years 1928-38 are as follows:

1928	43	1934	15
1929	107	1935	25
1930	na	1936	9
1931	na	1937	13
1932	68	1938	17
1933	68		

City of Montreal, *RASP,* 1928-39.

61. *Le Devoir,* 16 February 1922. Among the English-speaking population, the Montreal Day Nursery cared for children between six weeks and ten years old whose mothers were "forced to find work." In 1923, it took in 267 children from sixty-nine families, but their average stay was only five days.

62. *La Presse,* 14 January 1931.

63. *La Presse,* 28 July 1930; also 18 October 1930.

64. Bugeaud v. Dorion (1931), GP 7454. *Montreal Herald,* 22 July 1930. *Le Courrier de St-Hyacinthe,* 30 January 1931. *La Presse,* 21, 28 February 1931.

65. It was relatively easy in this period to adopt a minor child. Eligible for adoption were: (1) illegitimate children whose mother or father, or both, had not, in fact, taken charge of their care, expenses, and education or who had not declared in writing that they desired to do so; (2) orphans; (3) children whose parents were irremediably mentally incompetent; (4) children adopted by their maternal or paternal grandparents. *Statuts refondus de la Province de Québec,* 1925, d. 196, a.6, 3 Geo. VI, c. 85, a1.

66. See Chapter 6.

67. Archives of the Hôpital de la Miséricorde, correspondence in the medical files, 1935, 1937.

68. See n. 40.

69. Sylvie Côté, "L'oeuvre des orphelins de l'Hospice du Sacré-Coeur de Sherbrooke" (Master's thesis, University of Sherbrooke, 1987). Laurie Peel, "L'orphelinat Ste-Thérèse à Hull, 1928-1941," unpublished paper, History Department, University of Ottawa, February, 1982.

Chapter 6

1. M.E. Fleming and M. MacGillivray, *Fécondité de la femme canadienne, Septième Recensement du Canada,* 1931, 12 (Ottawa, 1936), p. 262.

2. Statistics compiled from the registers of the Hôpital de la Miséricorde, in the Archives of the Hôpital de la Miséricorde, Jacques Viger Hospital (AHM). For the Hôpital de la Miséricorde of Quebec City, run by the Sisters of the Good Shepherd, see Albert Jobin, "Hôpitaux de la Miséricorde et de la Crèche St-Vincent-de-Paul," *Bulletin de la Société Médicale des Hôpitaux Universitaires de Québec* (1934), p. 304.

3. Sr. Saint-Jean Vianney, SM, MSS, "Un peu d'histoire," paper presented at the Journée d'étude held on the occasion of the 10th anniversary of the incorporation of the Miséricorde social services (17 November 1955), pp. 4-5.

4. J.E. Dubé, "Nos hôpitaux. Leur passé, leur évolution, le présent," *L'Union médicale,* 61, 2 (February, 1932), pp. 179-80. In Quebec City, the Hôpital de la Miséricorde, under the direction of the Soeurs du Bon Pasteur, performed the same function as the hospital in Montreal and recorded an average of 457 deliveries a year between 1929 and 1933. See Jobin, "Hôpitaux de la Miséricorde," p. 304.

5. *Rapport annuel du Ministère de la Santé et du Bien-être social pour les années 1935 à 1941* (Quebec, 1944), p. 204.

6. AHM, C. Joncas to Sr. Tharcisius (20 February 1933); Sr. Tharcisius to Fr. B. (January, 1933).

7. AHM, 1929-1939.

8. AHM. Given the small percentage of factory workers who entered the Hôpital de la Miséricorde, it does not seem that illegitimacy was linked to industrial work, except to the degree that the industrial development of the towns encouraged an influx of young, unmarried women into the urban milieu. For a discussion of modernization and illegitimacy, see Edward Shorter, "Illegitimacy, Sexual Revolution, and Social Change in Modern Europe," *Journal of Interdisciplinary History,* 2, 2 (Autumn, 1971), pp. 237-72; J.W. Scott and L.A. Tilley, "Women's Work and the Family in Nineteenth Century Europe," *Comparative Studies in Society and History,* 17, 1 (January, 1975), pp. 36-64; J.R. Gillis, "Servants, Sexual Relations, and the Risks of Illegitimacy in London, 1800-1900," *Feminist Studies,* 5, 1 (Spring, 1979), pp. 142-73.

9. AHM. Mothers' and babies' weights are of little use in establishing the

state of health of these patients because they are rarely given. This lack of information prevents us from comparing our findings with those of Patricia Ward and Peter Ward in "Infant Birth Weight and Nutrition in Industrializing Montreal," *American Historical Review* (April, 1984).

10. Québec, Service provincial d'hygiène, *Rapport annuel,* 1928.

11. AHM.

12. AHM. The examples drawn from AHM are identified by the patient's file number, or the date, and if possible by both: #32653; #32771.

13. AHM.

14. AHM, 1932.

15. AHM. Sr. Tharcisius to A., #12637.

16. Arthur Prévost, *Toute la vérité sur la fille-mère et son enfant* (Montréal: Princeps, 1961), p. 46.

17. AHM, Sr. Tharcisius (30 September 1935, 21 October 1935, 7 November 1935).

18. NAC, Charlotte Whitton Papers, MG 30, E 256, Vol. 20, John Kerry, "The Legal Status of the Unmarried Mother and Her Child in the Province of Quebec" (1926).

19. Montreal, Judicial Archives, Sessions Court, Court of the King's Bench, 1929-39.

20. AHM (24 July 1937).

21. AHM (1933).

22. AHM (20 June 1936). A mother also wrote (2 March 1933) that as she had "relatives who were priests, cousins in religious orders in many Montreal communities," information must be given out to no one, "even a priest or a nun."

23. AHM, #35181 (10 May 1937).

24. AHM. A patient caught trying to send an uncensored letter had to serve an additional month, making a total of seven months after her confinement. #334502 (30 March 1936).

25. AHM. #32542 (1933).

26. AHM. As one mother from St. Hyacinthe wrote, "I wouldn't want to travel for nothing the time is too hard." #32000 (1933)

27. AHM. A blood transfusion was worth $20 or a month of service. #32357.

28. C.A. Décarie, "Malades mentales," *Annales Médico-chirurgicales de l'Hôpital Ste-Justine,* 1, 3 (May, 1932), p. 126.

29. AHM.

30. AHM (1939).

31. AHM, #32760 (17 October 1933). Similar requests on the part of patients' mothers may be found in #32357 (17 October 1933); #32578 (19 November 1933).

32. A seventeen-year-old "made a scene to avoid going and had to be taken by force." #35209 (May, 1937).

33. AHM, Sr. Tharcisius (18 August 1938).

34. AHM, Sr. Tharcisius (30 September 1935; 21 October 1935; 15 October 1937).

35. AHM (22 July 1938).

36. AHM (3 November 1937). Even a woman over the age of twenty-one might be kept against her will. To a hotel-keeper, who had brought his twenty-seven-year-old employee, an orphan, to the hospital, Sister Tharcisius wrote, "She wants to leave the hospital at all costs . . . she believes she is in prison. . . . If we keep her here it is only because of your clearly expressed desire." (#31557, 12 April 1932).

37. AHM, #32460 and #35175 (May, 1937). The woman still owed $97.

38. AHM, #32662 (1932).

39. #35436 (1935).

40. AHM (1932).

41. AHM. Sr. Tharcisius to the parish priest of St-Justine-de-Dorchester (18 April 1939).

42. AHM, #33660 (2 October 1935).

43. AHM. For having tried to send a clandestine letter, #34502 had to work an extra month at the crèche, serving a total of seven months after her confinement. Others punished for the same reason were #32771; #35217 (29 May 1937); #35840 (14 May 1938).

44. AHM, #33275 (1934); (May, 1939). Statistics compiled from the AHM registers.

45. AHM, #30621.

46. AHM. According to the records, she owed $97 to the hospital (#35175). In October, 1935, the police were called to put #34168 to bed.

47. Statistics compiled from AHM registers.

48. AHM, #36523 (9 October 1939). Gillis has shown that in nineteenth-century London, men who might have considered taking care of their girl friends and their children were often prevented by circumstances from doing so. Gillis, "Servants, Sexual Relations," pp. 157-163.

49. AHM, #30377 (18 February 1930).

50. AHM.

51. AHM, #32578 (19 November 1933).

52. AHM, Sr. Tharcisius to E.P. (15 July 1937).

53. AHM (2 March 1933).

54. *First Annual Report of the Women's Directory of Montreal* (Montreal, 1915).

55. *La Presse,* 13 January 1931.

56. Kerry, "Legal Status," pp. 9-10.

57. Quebec, Department of Municipal Affairs, Industry and Commerce, *Annuaire statistique du Québec, 1930-1940* (Quebec: King's Printer, 1931-1941).

58. Statistics compiled from AHM registers, 1929-39.
59. AHM. Statistics compiled from the registers of 1929-39. The crèches were
    extremely dangerous places to the lives of the babies. Dr. A. Jobin com-
    plained of the crowded conditions and unhealthiness of the crèche at the
    Hôpital de la Miséricorde in Quebec City. There, contagious diseases were
    devastating. In 1929, two-thirds of the 186 children taken there from Sacré
    Coeur Hospital in Quebec City were dead in a few months of whooping
    cough or measles. A. Jobin, "Historique d'une épidémie de rougeole à la
    crèche," *Bulletin médical de Québec,* 32 (1931), pp. 108-09. Venereal
    diseases transmitted by parents also claimed their victims. In 1928, there
    were eighty-seven children affected with syphilis and 516 with gonorrhea.
    Provincial Health Service, *Rapport annuel, 1928.*
60. AHM, 27 November 1939.
61. AHM, 1934. This type of comment appears more than once. For example,
    "Little Jeannine is dead. The Lord has been good enough to come and take
    her away, thanks be to God." 16 October 1935.
62. AHM, #35065.
63. AHM, #32364 (April, 1934, and 9 September 1934). The nuns were very
    aware of the rumours circulating regarding mistakes in identity at the
    crèche. In 1936, following a scandal in the United States, *La Revue
    moderne* printed a laudatory article about the Hôpital de la Miséricorde
    with the subtitle "Some babies switched in American maternity wards.
    Precautions taken to avoid these mistakes." See "A visit to the maternity
    ward," *La Revue moderne,* 15, 5 (March, 1936), pp. 30-31. All the same,
    the hero of *Soeur ou fiancée* is saved from an incestuous relationship
    because of a misunderstanding about his birth. de Cotret, *Soeur ou fiancée,*
    p. 56.
64. AHM, #32192 (April, 1933).
65. AHM (17 December 1956).
66. *Le Devoir,* 18 May 1937.
67. AHM, #31541 (April, 1932).
68. AHM, #34378. The woman had spent a year and a half at the Miséricorde.

Chapter 7

1. Robert A. Moreau, "Intempérance et prostitution à Hull, 1896-1914,"
   Outaouais, 1 (January, 1986), pp. 92-93. For a study of prostitution in
   Quebec before World War One, see Réjean Lemoine, "Maisons malfamées et prostitution," *Cap-aux-Diamants,* 1, 1 (Spring, 1985), pp.
   13-18.
2. *La Presse,* 18 May 1925.
3. At the Coderre Commission, Captain Sauvé of the Montreal police complained that charges against the houses of prostitution were routinely

dismissed and if the women pleaded not guilty, the police would lose their case. Coderre Commission, vol. 3, p. 2239.

4. Number 92 Cadieux was the most popular brothel after the war, with its three ballrooms, its piano player, and its large rear courtyard where the drivers of taxis and sleighs could wait for their fares while having a drink courtesy of Madame Russell. It would offer pornographic shows late into the night. It later moved to de Bullion Street. Coderre Commission, Hadick, vol. 1, pp. 528, 597; Sauvé, vol. 3, p. 2259; vol. 8, p. 7693; Geoffrion, vol. 8, p. 7693; Owen Dawson (who had a map of Montreal with red pins marking the brothel locations), vol. 1, pp. 428, 449.

5. *Le Monde ouvrier,* 6 July 1932.

6. Coderre Commission, Gauthier, vol. 2, pp. 989-90; Chief Pierre Bélanger, vol. 6, pp. 5728, 5731; Dawson, vol. 1, p. 443; Haywood, vol. 2, pp. 1173-75.

7. Ruth Rosen, *The Lost Sisterhood: Prostitution in America, 1900-1918* (Baltimore: Johns Hopkins University Press, 1981). In 1905, *La Presse* (27 January 1905) reported a traffic between Montreal and Valleyfield during the slack season in the textile industry and the state of New York. See also "La traite des blanches à Montréal," *Le Foyer* (1908); Rev. J.G. Shearer, "The Canadian Crusade," in Ernest A. Bell, *War on the White Slave Trade* (Toronto: Cole Publishing Co., 1980; reprint of 1911 edition), pp. 333-63.

8. *La Patrie,* 9, 10, 11, 13 February 1923.

9. *Montreal Daily Star,* 20 March 1923.

10. MJDM, Bricault v. Marchand, Côté, Ménard (1932), Sessions Court, GP 5284.

11. Bricaut v. Brown (1936).

12. Coderre Commission, Sauvé, vol. 8, p. 8433.

13. *Ibid.,* vol. 1, p. 784; vol. 3, p. 2321.

14. G. Lapierre, "L'adolescent à notre époque," *Annales Médico-chirurgicales de l'hôpital Ste-Justine,* 2, 3 (May, 1936), pp. 40-45.

15. Anna Herscovitch, widow of Sam Wax and companion of Tony Frank since 1924, rented the premises on Cadieux St. for this sum. Coderre Commission, vol. 3, p. 2438. Captain Sauvé explained the internal organization of the brothel to the Coderre Commission (vol. 3, 2233-35).

16. *Ibid.,* Dawson, vol. 1, p. 449.

17. Le Roi v. Lillian Hoover (24 February 1930), #3302, Police archives, Recorder's Court, Montreal.

18. Police archives, Recorder's Court. A review of forty-four arrest warrants issued against persons accused of running a bawdy house between 18 February and 13 March 1930. It is clearly impossible to establish whether Florida Carroll, Kathleen Wyman, Eva Wilson, Delia Baker, and Rose Campbell were all Anglophones.

19. Coderre Commission, vol. 1, pp. 447-49.

20. *Ibid.*, Herscovitch, vol. 3, p. 2433. In *Lovell's* street guide for 1924-25, she is named as occupying 315, 321, 323, and 331 Cadieux.

21. *Ibid.*, Dawson, vol. 1, pp. 449, 480. *Le Canada,* 14 March 1925.

22. Coderre Commission, vol. 8, pp. 6629-30.

23. *Ibid.*, Dawson, vol. 1, p. 447; Sauvé, vol. 3, p. 2320. Each stamp did not necessarily indicate another client. Those who wanted to stay longer paid again and the card would be punched accordingly.

24. *Ibid.*, Dawson, vol. 1, p. 461; Haywood, vol. 2, p. 1175.

25. *Ibid.*, Herscovitch, vol. 3, p. 2430.

26. *Ibid.*, Dawson, vol. 1, p. 460.

27. *Ibid.*, Gauthier, vol. 2, pp. 1011-12.

28. *Ibid.*, Haywood, vol. 2, p. 1161; vol. 8, p. 8151.

29. *Ibid.*, vol. 2, p. 1161. Cocaine was selling for $22 an ounce (p. 1167).

30. *Ibid.*, vol. 1, p. 734. MJDM, Cantin v. Labrecque (1932), Sessions Court, GP 10816.

31. *La Presse,* 3 April 1925.

32. Coderre Commission, Swail, vol. 3, p. 2328.

33. *Ibid.*, Geoffrion, vol. 7, pp. 7662, 7751. According to Lieutenant Grégoire of the morality squad, Rose Latour, alias Tremblay, called the police when some young men showed up in her house carrying drugs. (Grégoire, vol. 8, p. 6561.)

34. Or, more or less, Violet Fields, Blossom Meadows, and Lily of the Valley Woods. MJDM, Sessions Court and Court of the King's Bench, 1932, 1936-39.

35. Coderre Commission, Harris, vol. 3, p. 2596.

36. *Ibid.*, Geoffrion, vol. 8, p. 7699.

37. *Montreal Standard,* 24 March 1923.

38. Coderre Commission, Sauvé, vol. 7, pp. 6669, 6681.

39. Lloyd P. Gartner, "Anglo-Jewry and the International Traffic in Prostitution, 1885-1914," *Association of Jewish Studies Review,* 78 (1982-83), pp. 129-78. While observing that Anna Herscovitch was born in Russia in 1882, we do not know the circumstances that brought her from South Africa to Montreal in 1910. Coderre Commission, Herscovitch, vol. 3, pp. 2430-33.

40. *Ibid.*, Geoffrion, vol. 8, p. 7770.

41. *RASP,* Montreal, 1921-39. See Table 4.

42. Coderre Commission, Desloges, vol. 8, p. 7856.

43. *Ibid.*, pp. 7944-79.

44. *Ibid.*, Haywood, p. 7654; Archambault, vol. 8, pp. 7992, 8026. In 1920, 33 per cent of the female prisoners in Canada were infected with syphilis and 80 per cent with gonorrhea. Most of these women were in jail for sexual offences. Dr. Gordon Bates, "Essential Factors in a Campaign vs. Venereal Diseases," *Public Health Journal,* 12, 9 (September, 1921), p. 386. Dr. Desloges, who tended to exaggerate, informed the Commission that

between 60 and 70 per cent of the women in jail in Montreal for sexual offences had syphilis and 100 per cent had gonorrhea. (Coderre Commission, vol. 8, p. 7829.) Dr. Archambault made a distinction between the latent state and the active state of the disease, when the infected person is contagious. The police used the word "contagious" for everyone who tested positive.

45. Statistics cited before the Coderre Commission, vol. 8, p. 7738.

46. Erica-Marie Benadou, *La Prostitution et la Police des moeurs au XVIIIe siècle* (Paris: Perin, 1987), pp. 427-29.

47. Coderre Commission, Dawson, vol. 1, p. 468.

48. *Ibid.,* Geoffrion, vol. 7, p. 7611.

49. *Ibid.,* Desloges, vol. 7, p. 7844; Archambault, vol. 8, p. 8044; Haywood, vol. 8, pp. 8142, 8143; Conroy, vol. 8, pp. 8206-08.

50. *Ibid.,* Desloges, vol. pp. 7, 7756, 7829, 7833, 7907.

51. *Ibid.,* Dawson, vol. 1, p. 468.

52. *Ibid.,* Haywood, vol. 2, pp. 1155, 1156.

53. *Ibid.,* Dawson, vol. 1, pp. 441, 442.

54. *Ibid.,* Archambault, vol. 8, p. 8083.

55. Alain Corbin, *Les filles de noce Misère sexuelle et prostitution (19e siècle)* (Paris: Flammarion, 1982), p. 403.

56. Quebec, Provincial Health Service, *XIe Rapport annuel,* 1932-33, p. 112. Cassell, *The Secret Plague.*

57. Germain, *Le point d'interrogation,* p. 137.

58. Coderre Commission, Gauthier, vol. 2, p. 1013.

59. *Ibid.,* Swail, vol. 3, p. 2331.

60. When she was appearing before the Coderre Commission, her lawyer asked that the newspapers not report her testimony because she had daughters at a convent school (vol. 2, pp. 1100, 1101). Anna Herscovitch, Madame Anna, presented the same plea: "My Lord, please have mercy on my children, for I have honest children and this should not be put over on them, please" (vol. 3, p. 2443). The manager Lillian Vallée had two children boarding with a lady (vol. 7, p. 6562).

61. *Ibid.,* Haywood, vol. 2, p. 1166.

62. MJDM, Bugeaud v. Noël (1935).

63. Coderre Commission, Gregoire, vol. 4, p. 3689.

64. *Ibid.,* Haywood, vol. 2, p. 1151. *Montreal Daily Star,* 14 May 1925.

65. *Montreal Herald,* 17 January, 6, 8 February 1930.

66. Coderre Commission, Harris, vol. 3, pp. 2598, 2601, 2843; Hamel, vol. 7, pp. 6648, 6649.

67. MJDM, Sessions Court, #6818 (1933); #2453 (1931).

68. Coderre Commission, Senéchal, vol. 6, pp. 5124, 6728, 6729; Sauvé, vol. 3, pp. 2289-91. See note 33 above.

69. *Ibid.,* Harris, vol. 3, p. 2591.

70. MJDM, Cantin v. Labrecque (1932), Sessions Court, GP 10816, CBR, 1437, 1791, 2264, 4497.
71. Coderre Commission, Sauvé, vol. 3, pp. 2090, 2221, 2231, 2232; Lalonde, vol. 4, p. 3887.
72. *Ibid.,* Bélanger, vol. 1, pp. 861-63; David, vol. 2, p. 1105.
73. *Ibid.,* Haywood, vol. 2, p. 1169; Gauthier, vol. 2, p. 1013.
74. *Le Canada,* 4 March 1933.
75. *Le Devoir,* 3 February 1933. MJDM, Cantin v. Labrecque, Sessions Court, GP 10816.
76. Cantin v. Catton (1932), GP 10817. *Le Canada,* 3, 4 March 1933.
77. Bricault v. Mastrolorido (1937), GP 4280. Coderre Commission, vol. 2, pp. 1315-22, 1332.
78. MJDM, Cantin v. Catton (1932), GP 10817.
79. *Montreal Standard,* 3 March 1923.
80. The notion of controlling the health of prostitutes dates to the middle of the eighteenth century, three centuries after the first appearance of syphilis in European cities. See Benadou, pp. 427-29.
81. For the debate over suppression, see Andrée Lévesque, "Putting it Out."
82. Coderre Commission, Geoffrion, vol. 8, p. 7632.
83. Montreal, *RASP,* 1936-38. In 1936, 293 men and 2,202 women were examined; in 1937, 404 men and 2,452 women.
84. Montreal, *RASP,* 1920-39.
85. *Montreal Daily Star,* 9 April 1923.
86. Archives of Municipal Court, Recorder's Court.
87. Coderre Commission, Geoffrion, vol. 8, p. 7611.
88. *Montreal Daily Star,* 6 April 1923.
89. Coderre Commission, Sauvé, vol. 7, p. 6668.
90. Antoinette Hamel, alias Corbeil, also accused Captain Sauvé of having accepted a $50 bribe. *Ibid.,* pp. 6629-31.

Conclusion

1. *AC,* 1920-40.
2. *Le Canada,* 13 March 1931.

Index

Abortion, 78, 84-94, 138, 139; and social
     class, 91-92; among prostitutes, 122,
     127, 128, 158; cost of, 88; incidence
     of, 87, 137; means of producing,
     85-86; prosecutions for, 87, 89-90,
     93; sanctions against, 42
Adoption, 112, 114; decline in numbers
     of, 114
Adultery, 41, 66
Age of consent, 66
Alliance pour le vote des femmes, 16, 50,
     66
Americanization, 56
Anatomy as destiny, 12
Ante-mortem deposition, 84, 89, 91,
     94
Aquinas, Thomas, 36
Arcanum Divinae Sapientiae, 35
Archambault, Dr. Gustave, 125, 126
Archambault, Father Joseph-Papin, 15,
     19, 20, 29
Association catholique féminine, 72
Association des Gouttes de lait (Milk
     Drop Association), 46
Audollent, Bishop, 42
Audouin, Father, 24, 34
"Automobilism," 60

Bastien, Hermas, 44
Beaudoin, Dr. J.-A., 33, 44, 63
Beauvoir, Simone de, 12

Bégin, Cardinal Louis Nazaire, 37,
     50
Béïque, Senator Frédéric-Ligori, 55
Bélanger, Dr. Arthur, 55
Bélanger, Pierre, 129
Benadou, Erica-Marie, 125
Bennett, Richard, 104, 127
Bernard, Eva, 129
Bernier, Jovette, 55, 87
Bethune, Dr. Norman, 64
Bilodeau, Georges M., 44
Birth rate, 41, 50; decline in, 30, 76, 82,
     137
Bottle-feeding, 31; objections to on
     grounds of health, 31
Bourassa, Henri, 21, 40, 44, 49
Bourget, Bishop Ignace, 73, 102
Boyer, Judge, 71
Breach of promise, 67
Breast-feeding: as health issue, 31; as
     moral duty, 32
Bricault, Lieut. J.B., 128
Brossard, Mme. Edmond, 21
Brothels: and drugs, 123; and venereal
     disease, 125-26; conditions in,
     122-23; numbers of, 118;
     organization of, 121-23, 129;
     regulation of, 131; toleration of, 131
Brown, Alice, 123
Brown, Mamie (Eva Pilon), 121, 124,
     129

Broynard-Frot, Janine, 26
Bruchési, Mgr. P.N., 55, 70
Bruneau, Judge, 40

Cadron-Jetté, Rosalie, 73, 102
Cannon, Dr. O.A., 87
Casgrain, Thérèse, 50, 51
Casti Connubii, 27, 46
Catholic Church, 13; and abortion, 41, 42; and birth control, 27, 41; and breast-feeding, 31; and celibacy, 53; and censorship, 7; and divorce, 40; and motherhood, 27; and parental authority, 34; and rhythm method, 28, 83-84; and subjection of women, 35, 36, 37; as normative agency, 13
Catholic Film League, 71
Catton, Maurice, 130
Censorship: of film, 70; of literature, 71
Chapais, Senator Thomas, 41, 55
Chastity, 54; and seduction, 66; pre-marital, 65
Cherry, Jack, 41
Chevalier, Albert, 54
Child abandonment, 97-98, 137
Child Welfare Association, 33
Circé-Côté, Eva, 38, 58, 61, 69, 119, 131
Civil Code (Quebec), 40, 66
Clarté, 38
Clouthier, Father Émile, 43
Coderre, Judge, 68, 127
Coderre, Mme. Louis, 34
Coderre Police Commission, 63, 68, 86, 123, 125, 129, 130, 131, 133
Coitus interruptus, 83
"Colette," *see* Lesage, Édouardine
Committee of Sixteen, 68, 70
Committee on Moral Standards, 70
Communism and the family, 35
Communist press, 38
Condoms, 70, 84
Congregation of Notre Dame, 70
Contraception, 78, 82-84, 139; and eugenics, 30; laws forbidding, 41, 84; opposition to, 27
Cotret, Dr. René de, 55, 87, 93
Coubé, Canon Stéphane, 23, 38
Council of Trent, 53

Couture, Dr. Ernest, 87
Crèches, 97-98; private, 97
Criminal Code (Quebec), 67, 69, 106
Criminal Code (Canada), 41, 67, 95

Dancing as occasion of sin, 58
Daughters of Saint Marguerite, 112
David, Athanase, 23, 30, 45
Dawson, Owen, 87, 119, 126
Department of Health, Child Welfare Division, 29, 36
Derick, Carrie, 62, 63
Derrida, Jacques, 17
Desertion, 42
Désilets, Alphonse, 37
Desloges, Dr. Antoine-Hector, 19, 63, 125, 126, 127
Diaphragm, 84
Divorce, 40, 41
Domestics, 66, 102, 105, 114, 119, 121, 124, 133
Dorion, Judge C.E., 41
Dorion Commission, 66
Drugs in brothels, 123, 124
Dubois, Jeanne, 130, 131
Dufresne, Fernand, 130, 137
Duplessis, Maurice, 19, 44
Dupuis, Mme. F.-X., 57
Duquette, Mayor Charles, 68

École sociale populaire, 35
Education: domestic science, 37, 45, 48, 49; father's role in, 36; for marriage and motherhood, 27, 45; higher, for girls, 37, 38, 45, 48; of girls, 45
Emigration, 18, 30
Employers: sex with employees a criminal offence, 66
Eugenics, 27, 30, 62
Evanik, Mrs. George, 51
Excommunication, 41
Extramarital affairs, 55

"Fadette," *see* Saint-Jacques, Henriette Dessaulles
Family: economic role of, 21; government interference in, 21; perceived decline of, 20

Family allowance, 43-44
Fashion, 56-58; and social class, 58; as moral danger, 58
Fédération nationale Saint-Jean-Baptiste (FNSJB), 16, 34, 35, 37, 43, 48, 50, 57, 68, 70, 72; and women's suffrage, 50
Female criminality, 75, 79
Feminism, 51, 65; and motherhood, 38; attacks on, 37, 50
Flandrin, Jean-Louis, 13
Fontaine, Dr. R., 85
Fortin, Joseph-Édouard, 50
Foucault, Michel, 7, 13
Fournier, Charles, 50
Francq, Gustave, 38, 69, 131
Frank, Tony, 122, 123
Fréchette-Handfield, Pauline, 14

Gagnier, Dr. L.-A., 65
Gangsters and prostitution, 128
Garçonnisme, 60
Gauthier, Mgr. Georges, 34
Gauthier, Father Henri, 63, 68, 70, 119, 123, 127
Gauthier, Dr. Pierre, 50
Gauvreau, Dr. Joseph, 33
Geoffrion, Judge Amédée, 61, 65, 69, 124, 132, 133
Gérin-Lajoie, Dr. Léon, 28, 87
Gérin-Lajoie, Marie Lacoste, 48, 68
Gérin-Lajoie, Sr. Marie, 24, 35
Germain, Father Victorin, 26, 28, 42, 54, 61, 72, 127
Gidlow, Elsa, 80
Godbout, Adélard, 19
Gordon, Nathan, 63
Gouin, Lomer, 19
Great Depression, 19, 21, 42, 48, 76, 87, 91, 114, 136, 137; and prostitution, 121, 127; and venereal disease, 127
Grey Nuns, 48, 97, 102
Groulx, Father Lionel, 136

Hachette, R., 38
Halle, Beatrice Forbes-Robertson, 21
Hamilton, Mrs. Henry, 46

Harbour, Canon, 71
Harris, Flora, 124, 128, 129
Harvey, Jean-Paul, 71
Haywood, Dr. Alfred K., 63, 119, 121, 123, 125, 126, 127
Herscovitch, Anna, 122, 123, 124, 127
Hoover, Lillian, 122, 128, 129
Hôpital de la Miséricorde of Montreal, 16, 17, 62, 72, 78, 98, 101, 124, 138; origins of, 73, 102
Hôpital de la Miséricorde of Quebec City, 73, 101
Hull, 120

Illegitimacy, rate of, 101
Infant mortality, 33, 45, 113; high rate in Montreal, 113; in Hôpital de la Miséricorde, 113; mothers' responsibility for, 33
Infanticide, 94-97; incidence of, 95
Influenza epidemic, 20, 53

Jesuit religious pamphleteering, 13
Jeune Canada, 29
Jeunesse ouvrière catholique, 46

L'Action française, 21, 29, 44, 71
L'Action libérale nationale, 136
L'Aide à la Femme, 72
L'Amour de la carte postale, 74
La Bonne Parole, 14, 16, 31, 57, 61
Labrecque, Joseph, 123, 129, 130
La Chair décevante, 55, 87
Lachapelle, Dr. Séverin, 46
Lalande, Father Louis, 29
L'Almanach de la langue française, 52
La Patrie, 97, 117
Lapierre, Dr. Gaston, 27, 29, 33, 41
La Presse, 21, 42, 45, 98
La Sphère féminine, 16
Laurier Palace fire, 70-71
League for Women's Rights, 50
League of Catholic Women, 21
Le Canada, 21
Lebel, Léon, 43
Le Devoir, 49
Le Foyer, 72
Le Monde ouvrier, 16, 61, 69, 119, 131

Leo XIII, 35
Le Sage, Dr. Albert, 14
Lesage, Édouardine, 24
Lesbians, 76, 80, 117
Les Demi-Civilisés, 71
Letellier, Judge R., 86
Lévesque, Albert, 52
Levitsky, Annie, 130
Liberal Party, 137
Ligue des Bonnes Moeurs (Morality
    League), 55
Ligue des Femmes chrétiennes, 70
Liguori, Saint Alphonsus, 53
Longpré, Dr. Daniel, 32
L'Ouvrier canadien, 38

MacMurchy, Helen, 23, 36
Madelon, 112
Maison Sainte-Domitille, 73
Maison Sainte-Hélène, 73
Malthusianism, 28
Margueritte, Victor, 60
Marriage, 53; indissolubility of, 40;
    purpose of, 53
Marriage preparation courses, 46
Marriages, mass, 46
Martin, Claire, 60
Martin, Father Henri, 28
Martin, Médéric, 69, 131
Mastrolorido, Angelo, 130
Masturbation, 80; female, 54; male, 54
Maurault, Father Olivier, 27
Medical publications: social influence of,
    14
Medicine: normative role of, 14
Mercier, Dr. L.P., 27
Midwives, 33
Monpetit, Edouard, 21
Monpetit Commission, *see* Royal
    Commission on Social Services
Montreal General Hospital, 64, 119, 123,
    126
Montreal Health Service, 95, 97
Montreal Local Council of Women
    (MLCW), 62, 68, 70, 132
Montreal Society for the Protection of
    Women and Children, 42
Montreuil, Gaëtane de, 45

Movies: and nationalist groups, 71; as
    occasion of sin, 60; morality of, 71

National Congress of Child Welfare, 21
Naturalism, 60
Noël, Alphonse, 84, 88, 128

Ogino-Knauss, *see* Rhythm method
Ouellette-Michalska, Madeleine, 74

Pailleur, Canon, 46
Palmer, Dorothea, 28, 83
Panneton, Father, 60
Paquet, Canon Louis-Adolphe, 36, 37, 52
Pautrier, Dr. L.-M., 61
Pimps, 128; and the police, 130
Pinard, Dr. Adolphe, 28
Pius IX, 41, 46
Pius XI, 60
Point d'Interrogation, 42
Police: relations with prostitutes, 128
Police brutality; against prostitutes, 128
Police corruption, 128-29
Premarital pregnancy, 54; fictional
    treatment of, 55
Preparation for marriage courses, 46
Prévost, Dr. J.M.E., 64
Prostitution: abolition of, 68; and disease,
    64, 65, 69, 125-27; and double
    standard, 66; and feminism, 67; and
    illiteracy, 63; and mental deficiency,
    63; and poverty, 63; as consequence
    of parental negligence, 61;
    legalization of, 68; regulation of, 67,
    69; toleration of, 68
Provincial Health Service (Quebec) 64
Psychoanalysis and sexuality, 13
Public pools as occasion of sin, 59

Rape, 128; prosecutions for, 67
Red-light district, 62, 68, 70, 78, 117
Refuge du Bon Pasteur, 73
Refuge Ste-Pélagie, 102
"Revenge of the Cradle," 29
Revue dominicaine, 56
Revue Moderne, 10
Rhythm method, 28, 83-84
Ritchie-England, Grace, 68, 74

Roles within marriage, 35-36

Rourke, Maria, 72

Roy, Ferdinand, 45

Roy, Father Henri, 46

Roy, Mgr., 49

Royal Commission of Inquiry into Laurier Palace fire, 71

Royal Commission on Social Services, 43, 112

Russell, Lillian (Mme. Balthazar Scheller), 121, 124

Saint-Jacques, Henriette Dessaulles, 24, 27, 29, 45, 50

Saint-Jean, Idola, 50, 51, 112

Saint-Michel, Julien, *see* Circé-Côté, Eva

Saint-Pierre, Arthur, 54

Salvation Army, 103

Sanger, Margaret, 83

Sauvé, Arthur, 30

Sauvé, Captain Roch, 63, 128, 129, 133

Seduction: of minors, 65; prosecutions for, 66

Semaines sociales du Canada, 15, 20, 27, 40, 41, 45, 50

Semple, Judge, 133

Sex education, 72; absence of, 60

Smart, Patricia, 26

Social class, 11, 13, 16, 21, 58, 91-92, 103

Soeur ou fiancée, 55, 87, 93

Soeurs du Bon-Conseil, 24

Soeurs du Bon-Pasteur d'Angers, 72, 108, 109, 121

Street prostitution, *see* Streetwalkers

Streetwalkers: and venereal disease, 127; and violence, 128

Swail, John, 123, 127

Swimming as occasion of sin, 60

Szasz, Thomas, 77

Taschereau, Alexandre, 19, 51

Tassé, Henriette, 26, 30, 37

Tharcisius, Sr., 105, 106, 108, 109, 110, 112, 114, 116

Trades and Labour Congress of Canada (TLC), 38

Tremblay, Chief Joseph, 63

Tuberculosis as cause for legal abortion, 91

Turcotte, Father Dominique Augustin, 35

Ubi Arcano, 19

Unemployment, 21, 34; and prostitution, 131

Union Nationale, 19, 136

Unions, 16; and image of women, 38; women's role in, 51

Unmarried women: social expectations of, 25; and prostitution, 64, 69

Vagrancy, teenage, 121

Venereal disease, 61, 69, 125-27, 132-35; among Miséricorde patients, 103; control of, 69

Viau, Delina, 84

Vie ouvrière, 38

Vien, Thomas, 41

Virginity: as ideal, 53; loss of, 55

White slave trade, 64, 67, 72, 119-21

Wilson, Judge Charles, 86, 96

Winter sports as occasion of sin, 58

Women's Directory of Montreal, 112

Women's suffrage, 15, 30, 50, 55, 78, 137; and fears for the birth rate, 50

THE CANADIAN SOCIAL HISTORY SERIES

Terry Copp,
The Anatomy of Poverty: The Condition of the Working Class in Montreal 1897-1929, 1974.

Alison Prentice,
The School Promoters: Education and Social Class in Mid-Nineteenth Century Upper Canada, 1977.

John Herd Thompson,
The Harvest of War: The Prairie West, 1914-1918, 1978.

Joy Parr, Editor,
Childhood and Family in Canadian History, 1982.

Alison Prentice and Susan Mann Trofimenkoff, Editors,
The Neglected Majority: Essays in Canadian Women's History, Volume 2, 1985.

Ruth Roach Pierson,
"They're Still Women After All": The Second World War and Canadian Womanhood, 1986.

Bryan D. Palmer,
The Character of Class Struggle: Essays in Canadian Working Class History, 1850-1985, 1986.

Alan Metcalfe,
Canada Learns to Play: The Emergence of Organized Sport, 1807-1914, 1987.

Marta Danylewycz,
Taking the Veil: An Alternative to Marriage, Motherhood, and Spinsterhood in Quebec, 1840-1920, 1987.

Craig Heron,
Working in Steel: The Early Years in Canada, 1883-1935, 1988.

Wendy Mitchinson and Janice Dickin McGinnis, Editors,
Essays in the History of Canadian Medicine, 1988.

Joan Sangster,
Dreams of Equality: Women on the Canadian Left, 1920-1950, 1989.

Angus McLaren,
Our Own Master Race: Eugenics in Canada, 1885-1945, 1990.

Bruno Ramirez,
On the Move: French-Canadian and Italian Migrants in the North Atlantic Economy, 1860-1914, 1990.

Mariana Valverde,
"The Age of Light, Soap, and Water": Moral Reform in English Canada, 1885-1925, 1991.

Bettina Bradbury,
Working Families: Age, Gender, and Daily Survival in Industrializing Montreal, 1993.

Andrée Lévesque,
Making and Breaking the Rules: Women in Quebec, 1919-1939, 1994.